Finding Your True Self

Finding Your True Self

FINDING A PATH TO THE FLOURISHING LIFE YOU ENVISIONED FOR YOURSELF

Dr. Paul Serwinek

ISBN (paperback): 979-8-88759-399-9

ISBN (ebook): 979-8-88759-400-2

YOUR FREE RESOURCE

A FREE 15 MINUTE PHONE CONVERSATION WITH THE AUTHOR.

I would be happy to meet with any of my readers who send in a short review of my book to Amazon. We can discuss any question you have on concepts found in my book or your personal next steps leading to a fulfilling life.

As you read this book, please take a minute to send a comment on my book, hopefully a positive review or a constructive thought for my future publications.

IF YOU COULD…PLEASE take a minute to go to Amazon or wherever you purchased this book to register your review. I will then set up a time to meet with you. This will be a great help to me and much appreciated!

Paul

Table of Contents

PREFACE

Discovering Your True Self

I am finding many of us have been living with ourselves for years but still do not really know who we are. When asked to talk about ourselves we normally refer to our occupation like accountant, carpenter or mother. Maybe we refer to our gender or age, but those descriptions just scratch the surface. Often, we begin thinking of ourselves as only one or two of those aspects. I began thinking of myself as a student, then a husband, then a father etc. Yet, I was much, much more. My research proves that individuals who really know themselves have a much happier, more satisfying and successful life wherever they decide to go with their futures. To help you make that journey to finding who you are from many perspectives I have written this guide. This volume includes many of the topics seekers find invaluable while discovering who they really are. I can promise you, if you read through the chapter topics, you will find topics you have struggled with and questioned. I and many other philosophers, community leaders, theologians and successful leaders have gone through this same process. I can attest that any one of these topics will get you to thinking about your life and where it is going. The first, and one of the most critical abilities to learn, if you have not already learned, is how to think from a from a higher plane and broader outlook. For want of a better term I call this "thinking with a spiritual perspective." (I am not necessarily talking about a religious level here). By going into a life search with an open mind and not a cynical mind you will be surprised to find new perspectives and different outlooks you may never have dreamed possible. Imagine finding answers to questions you have for ages been searching for. Have you ever sensed the feeling that something is missing from your life? Examine your personal life outlook, wherever you are now, with a calm heart and an open mind and you will find the peace of mind you have longed for and everyone deserves to attain.

Many in our modern, science-oriented society consider themselves merely a product of their DNA. But again, we are much more, a being with a mind unique and an individual viewpoint and a product of an environment only you have experienced. You have feelings and emotions unique to you depending on your life circumstances and history. In addition, the ancient Greeks posited a separate SOUL placed within a separate self and that soul being the true self. Even centuries before the Greeks, the Hebrews used a term translated into English as "soul" also but meaning one's true being and not necessarily a separate entity within one's body but perhaps one's total being including mind, heart (feelings) and more. This entity is one's true self, one's true being or one's "soul" (not necessarily the Greek version of the term). To feel one is in touch with the "True Me" is a gratifying feat. To know for certain what you have been born or designed for gives one an advantage. To know what our DNA and life circumstances have prepared us for, these are all issues we need to wrestle with. And here is one of the big ones, and you probably never even thought about yet, is a question everyone needs to answer if they ever are to find what is that missing something in one's life: How do I balance the desire to feel good about myself and feel useful helping others with the equal need to protect myself from injury and insure my survival, both needs of which my whole being is begging me to resolve? That is a real balancing act!

My premise for this volume is that getting back in contact with one's true self, including all that makes you, you, will allow each of us to truly know ourselves and allow you to become fully aware of who, what and why you are. Knowing your true 'being" permits you to be in touch with what you really want deep down inside, what activities will give long-term meaning to your lives and what feelings will allow you to sense you are living fully. In a word, we want to feel we are living a "Flourishing Life." Yet, what is flourishing to us will be different for each person depending on who he or she really is deep down in "being." Getting in touch with true being allows each of us to find what may be a new more appealing occupation, building more fulfilling relationships and finding activities and circumstances that create far-reaching life satisfaction. You will be able to live in surroundings that promote more ongoing enjoyment, not just fleeting, very occasional moments of joy. For example, it took me till age thirty to realize I was a philosopher at heart. I had lived twelve years out of high school making a decent living but with very limited life satisfaction. I had listened to peers and elders surrounding me telling me how I SHOULD live MY life. Only when I began to know myself did I decide to go to college, first for a bachelor's degree, then a master's and finally my PhD in Sociology and Social Psychology. I had started out finding myself only after getting married, becoming a father, and working full time in an unfulfilling job. I lost years of productive time not knowing myself first. But, no regrets, I have learned after forty plus years since then, it is never too late to, in earnest, begin asking, "Who am I really?" It was not easy having made the mistake of putting the cart before the horse in my life, raising a family before raising myself, but, I surely enjoyed the next life period, working hard because I was doing what my true being expected of me!

A second mission for my book is the importance of realizing there is knowledge, wisdom and understanding available to us over and above what we see, hear, touch. Many would have us believe these are the only avenues of procuring understanding about ourselves, about our natural world and the social system we find ourselves surrounded and influenced by. Those of us who admit we have emotions, feelings, instincts and insights that well up from within and then analyze those, acknowledge they have added resources available in searching for meaning and our unique purpose that comes with knowing our true selves. Consider, we all have experienced what is referred to as "serendipity." A spiritual person finds that happening quite often. Just yesterday my wife, Marlene, was attempting to help a friend with a serious conflict. She had no idea where to start. Having to start somewhere, she called a possible number, the wrong number. Yet that "wrong" number connected her to the right person who just happened to be there at the time. This primary contact then mentioned the person who could possibly provide the help requested and, in fact, just happened to be coming that day. "She will be able to help your friend." I believe all of us have had that experience at times. Of course, a doubter will say, "That's just probability based on statistics and numbers prove this will help occasionally by chance." But when it happens on a regular basis to some, that is not just chance. A spiritual person learns to accept such phenomena. When I use the term "spiritual" I am not necessarily talking in religious terms.

Regularly, someone with a spiritual disposition will find herself finding an idea just "happens" to pop into her mind that seems to be the preferred solution for a person's distressing predicament. This is intuition. How it works, why it works has not been discovered yet but believing it works seems to provide the impetus to allow the mechanism to operate more freely. Again, statistically this cannot be proved since a spiritually minded person cannot just "will" an event to occur whenever desired. By the same token, I cannot say to a person who regularly senses such providential "chance" encounters, "This is just your imagination." What we do have is an anecdotal account that does bear witness to validity of their experiences. I encourage the reader to be aware of such "coincidences" happening in his or her life.

A third idea I highlight in this text is a refutation of the notion first proposed by the philosopher John Locke in the Eighteenth Century. He suggested we humans come into this world with a "Clean Slate" or "Tabula Rosa." In other words, he asserted all we know has been imparted to us by other humans, by parents or community around us. This is simply not true, even though to this day many scientists conduct their research with such assumptions. There are indeed concepts humans are born with, built within. An example is the concept of "cause and effect." No one has to teach a child this principle. A baby in short order "knows" this intuitively. Even a month or so after birth, if touched or whispered to, the child will soon turn her head to look to see what caused that touch or sound. A child need not be trained to look for what caused those various experiences, she inherently senses to expect a reason for an action or the cause for any phenomenon. Another good example to consider might be something more complex like the concept of Justice and Fairness. As a parent I did not need to train my children to distinguish when someone was being treated unfairly, they readily sensed what was happening and felt within their gut the act was "wrong." Further, every civilization, no matter how remote, has prohibitions regarding social aspects of living and they are remarkably similar regardless of the remoteness of the tribe or the age of a civilization. A seeker taught to accept and use the gifts built within him or her is a step ahead of a peer never taught to respect the treasure built within and they are absolutely free gifts. I encourage my readers to humbly admit his human mind and nervous system comes programmed, if you will, in finite ways. The minds and systems given us were to make sense of the world but limited, limited in capacity and limited in capability. To insist we humans can predict the ramifications of any decisions we make for years down the horizon or to predict all the possible variables that might explain an event about to occur or all the resulting consequences possible is wishful thinking. We must admit our limitations individually and as a society. Let us use our gifts gratefully and judiciously and realize there are times we must look beyond ours and other human's finite minds.

And here is one little caution to be aware of when reading here. You know or should realize that all of us speak based on our own personal subconscious assumptions. It should be only fair that a writer divulges his perspective. Most scientists, for instance, start with this assumption that all events in nature can be explained by material or physical factors of some sort. This is an assumption which, of course, can never be proved true, only accepted based on one's disposition. There is nothing wrong with that as long as the scientist states that assumption in advance or is conscious of it personally, no problem. By the same token, I write with an awareness that there are non-material forces in the universe that a physical mind or body may not be able to detect. Again, this cannot be proved true beyond doubt, similar to the scientist's acceptance, but I divulge mine in advance. I do not expect you to accept my position but only that you respect it as a viable option. I also have been trained as a philosopher, a theologian and a sociologist so my background will explain my world views. I would hope that would lend credence to what I am about to report. I have studied, researched and experienced life with these lenses for many decades now. So, I would hope that after expending that effort I have arrived at, at least, some discoveries worth my passing on.

And this acknowledgement goes for my own Christian world view also. Over the years I have had to modify frequently and temper my views on morality, justice and approach to life to keep up with new discoveries, new ideas and entirely new perspectives. I would like to think I am a seeker of truth and am obligated to admit where past views were inadequate to explain contradictions in beliefs. I am willing to admit my past errors and how life experience has a way of teaching us by our errors. I have come to find, though, that most of my fellow humans agree with me on the majority of the realities of life, that is, if they were forced to commit themselves to have to make a decision. All societies have sanctions on murder (and what is defined as murder), lying, stealing, sexual activity, on and on regardless of religion or lack thereof. There are also vast similarities in world religions and secular laws to the concepts of Christianity. So, when I appeal to Christian principles on occasion in this manuscript to explain a concept, I am employing it with the understanding that the principle is substantiated by other ancient manuscripts from other religions and other philosophies. There is something to be said for ideas that have stood the test of time. And while I have studied religions extensively, I have specialized in Western thought so I am quite conversant in that arena and use those ideas as a starting point with the understanding that identical examples can be cited from other religions and communities as well. My motive is not to attempt to convert the reader to my persuasion other than to establish that the Christian system (and perhaps other systems) really does work to explain life and living in a most adequate way. I am not ever mentioning specific doctrines in my writing here but only examining universe principles. For example, life teaches us there are consequences for all our actions. This is a basic principle of living. Some Christians like to stress the consequences on the punishment side of the ledger and stress the concept by appealing to the condition called Hell or Hades first introduced in Greek mythology. It is a popular concept in many settings though most Christians do not believe in a literal Hellfire as the non-Christian Greeks conceived the condition. Doctrines in any religion or political institution (Communism or Capitalism) are expected to change. However, the basic principle remains constant.

That is what this volume stresses, the principles for living that lead to a successful, satisfying and flourishing life. I have stumbled upon a set of such principles found in Christianity but closely linked to such principles found in other sources, other philosophies, other research studies, other historical data and personal interviews with individuals of countless backgrounds I have met spanning the over sixty years of my relentless studies. In fact, Christianity, the philosophy I began to study for ideas on my quest for the best way to live, was originally conceived and thought of as a "WAY OF LIFE." The original practitioners thought the tenets to be the best possible way to live a life. Principles like Love, Trustworthiness, Loyalty, Goal setting, Perseverance, Justice, Optimism, on and on. All readers will be familiar with these but may have never thought through the real-world consequences of not employing them and that will perhaps motivate readers to work to perfect them.

You will find here chapters on some of the basic questions that I feel all of us should contemplate at some point. Questions like, Why are we Here? Which concept of God is the most practical? Why, if there is a benevolent Higher Power, would he allow suffering? Is this life all there is? And others. I would like to welcome and introduce you to what many scholars, teachers, saints, intellectuals and martyrs have taught me and millions of others along with the work I have done over many years to make these ideas compatible with our modern world. I am always open to questions and comments on what is written here. I do not presume to have all the answers but starting with this wisdom, the readers will have a sixty-year head start toward their personal project of growth. This is a fascinating study that has kept me engrossed for all these years. And do contact me if you are a seeker looking for assistance. I also would love to hear from you if you have already found the answers you have been looking for. I wish you well in your journey.

Chapter 1

Spirituality Has Relevance In Our Modern World

Like never before it seems our society is having a difficult time deciding what our core beliefs should be. Most, I think, will agree something is especially missing in our modern world. My premise is that since many people have lost trust in our long- standing institutions whether political, religious or even science oriented, we are in dire need of a fresh perspective. I will not even comment on the political turmoil the world finds itself mired in. Similarly, religion in general has failed to excite many young people, and, in fact, people of all demographic categories. To me that is an indication religion, as such, is not presenting the answers to the question people are currently asking. And now science has been called into question with the contradictory interpretation of scientific data on treating Covid the last few years. Seekers are searching for a clear theme around which to build a life. They want a clear meaning for their lives and relevant, practical answers as to how to go about living a happy life that won't backfire on them in the future. "Happy" to them means relevance, excitement, comfortable existence. What appears to be true is that searchers, especially young and unbiased searchers, need something more than rules, laws and procedures. First, they want answers that are relevant, clear and uncontradictory to the questions they are asking.

I intend on demonstrating that a good starting point for our discussion is searching for answers from a Spiritual, not religious perspective. Spirituality, though sometimes mentioned from a religious viewpoint is NOT what I am talking about here. Spirituality is a way of analyzing data and ideas that will help a seeker to better comprehend political, social, religious or scientific arguments to take meaningful positions. For example, as stated above, religion is no longer considered relevant by many. Doctrine is not relevant to them. Studies about, or as I call it, speculation about What God is? What is the Hereafter? Does God punish people, or do they punish themselves? are great debate issues. But those answers are not what seekers are asking for. People, especially the young, want practical answers to questions about living now. Questions like, what are the ingredients to a happy life? How do I make my life more exciting and interesting? What is required for me to have more career and job satisfaction? How do I make decisions, so they won't come back to haunt me? On and on. I know from my own half century of searching, those questions can be simply answered and answered with content that is understandable, reasonable and acceptable to most who are working through life, whether they are religious, secular, agnostic or those who have deferred making any decisions as yet. The answer is Spirituality, the ability to think outside the box, the ability to always be open to new ideas and not stubbornly hanging on to methods that have never really worked in the first place.

I start here by reviewing my definition of Spirituality. I reiterate this definition is not an inclusive one and perhaps an unduly lengthy one. There will always be problems with word meaning and semantics and this definition is always open to editing and revising. This is merely a means of communication and a basis for discussion: Spirituality is simply the attitude and practice of seeking inspiration, guidance and understanding for effective living from all possible sources and evaluating ideas without preconceived notions or prejudice. I can also say Spirituality is a way to enhance AWARENESS of the universe. And for those who have an aversion to the word Spirituality, I would use the phrase "An Abstract, boundaryless and Non-discriminatory Awareness and Imagination" as a secular substitute.

More specifically, Spirituality is a personal search for understanding human existence, meaning and purpose using all resources available. The resources include objective mental intelligence and subjective emotional intelligence along with feelings that include intuition and subconscious inspiration and gut sensations.

The goal is to find oneself, then to like oneself and experience harmony with the physical world, with personal relationships and with the non-material, intangible world of ideas and realms beyond humanity's limited senses, without denying possibilities beyond immediate perception. Seekers use all these resources to flourish and become all that they can become as humans, recognizing their connection with all in the Universe and a sense there is something more immense to human existence than personal self.

(You will note, this definition does not restrain one by limiting science, sensory or religious input.)

In addition to the usual five senses, we allow ourselves to employ intuition, creativity, subjective feelings and even mystical sensations to make sense out of reality. I affirm in this piece we are able to find answers to subjective questions like: Who am I? What is the purpose of human existence? Is there meaning in human existence? This ability gives thinking humans a method to find answers to life questions that provide a more complete picture of a human world and are the bases of many higher order questions. Spirituality includes a search for abstract understanding that may not be answerable by science or pure rationality alone. Spirituality suggests a connection of all aspects with all other aspects within our universe. A good example is any one of myriads of questions connected with "Justice" and equitable solutions, currently in the news daily. Rationality or reasoning with a scientific background could never answer such questions. Science, being a study of objective rather than subjective issues, cannot determine the correct choice in personal matters. A personal choice has a desired result but that desired outcome is a personal choice. When talking personal preference, we are no longer in the realm of science. Subjective questions often can have many more than one right answer. However, starting with a spiritual viewpoint, can provide better answers and more readily, as we will demonstrate.

So, Spirituality is our personal way of orienting ourselves to the world around us. The opposite of this is living life without direction, excitement or meaning. And by this I am intending to show, a spiritual life is one with flourishing, growth, and positive results that induce the actor to cherish being alive. That is the way I try to live! Not living by rote or by status quo but living with exciting goals ahead. Is that not the kind of life we all long for? Therefore, a spiritual life course is not exactly the same for each of us. Our lives are uniquely based on heredity, DNA, Life Experience, Early Training, Personality and other factors. I can almost guarantee, if you let your mind soar, your desires ferment, then your path will open to new ideas and suggestions, fascinating and out of the ordinary thoughts that seem to arrive from nowhere in particular will start generating. You soon come to find who you are and what your abilities and circumstances intend for you to do. Some would say those intensions are what God planned for us personally and that may be just another way of explaining the same concept. Either way, the seeker will soon find, based on the unique person he really is, his possible true calling. However the reader would want to describe this concept, be my guest. Regardless, you are who you are, unique in all the world.

While it is true each of us needs to accept the responsibility to find out for ourselves who we really are, the task is not very difficult. We need only be honest with ourselves. Start asking, "What do I enjoy doing? What talents do I have? What am I good at? What are the hobbies I enjoy, and did I pick them or did someone else pick for me? What about when I was in school, what subjects did I enjoy the most?" Write down your answers. Within a few days you will know more about yourself than you thought you did.

This exercise will give you answers to subjective questions like: Who am I? What is the purpose of human existence? Is there meaning in human existence? This ability gives thinking humans a method to find answers to life questions and also then gives humans a more complete picture of our human world. Spirituality includes a search for what cannot be answered by science or pure rationality. Spirituality assumes a connection of all parts with all other parts within our universe. A good example of what I am claiming is found in any one of myriads of questions that science or rationality could never answer. One of the major issues in our civilization is connected with finding Fairness and Justice for all members. For instance, this current debate, how does our society give minority students priority in getting into top colleges without discriminating against other minority students brought up in a culture that insists children be taught to compete vigorously to be successful in education? Asian and Indian students feel they are being discriminated against. There are too many variables present complicating any determination of an equitable solution. Rationality or reasoning with a scientific background could never answer such a question. Science, being a study of objective rather than subjective issues, cannot determine the correct choice in personal matters. Can we prove that a poor student must be given priority over a middle-class status student? A personal choice may have an outcome or end result desirable but that end result is again very personal. When talking personal preference, we are no longer in the realm of science. Subjective questions deal with personal choice and choices can have many more than one right answer. However, a spiritual viewpoint can readily answer such questions as we will see as we tread on.

To help in understanding this idea of spirituality and the desperate need of it, I am going to cite several verses of Jesus' words that I hope will make matters clearer. Here Jesus is not talking from a religious perspective. Christianity had not been originated as a religious institution yet when Jesus spoke. In fact, Christianity was originally referred to simply as "The Way" (Acts19:9). What later became institutionalized as a religion started out as a "Way of Life." Jesus had clarified moral reasoning and removed the inconsistencies that created moral dilemmas going back some four thousand years even before Jesus' day. When he came on the scene, the masses were living with behaviors that were preventing their communities from engaging in a fulfilling life. Jesus addressed those errors.

The first verse I highlight here is Matthew 5:3. "Blessed are the poor in spirit, for theirs is the Kingdom of Heaven." In so many words Jesus was saying EVERYONE CAN BE PART OF God's

Family (The Kingdom of Heaven). Translated into non-religious terms, anyone can have a sublime or close to ideal life even if they come with a "poor spirit." The problem is, per Jesus, most people live a life lacking in spirit, "a poor spirit." They are living life with a minimum of "human spirit" or the "team spirit" that the human race should be living and sharing. All humans hail from the same ancestry, all are related, all bound and constructed with the same DNA. All are striving for the same things, primarily survival and to be "happy," which can be interpreted in various ways. What Jesus says is missing for many of us is a meaning and purpose in life that gives direction and excitement. Yet, I have lived long enough to see how human team spirit, like patriotic spirit, changes over time. I have lived through periods when US Patriotic Spirit was very high, then very low, then high again, a number of times. I lived as a child, after World War II when our US society was very patriotic. That was the time when Superman on TV was proud to believe in the "American Way." But my generation, The Baby Boomers, fought in Vietnam and our soldiers came back from war, and in general, came back disillusioned and were spat upon by many of my peers. Patriotic spirit was quite low. Then Ronald Reagan and the Moral Majority gained the ascendency and patriotism was in style again. However, that did not last barely a generation when a more liberal element of our society began rethinking our constitutional heritage. Soon our American heroes for some two hundred years like Washington, Jefferson, Lincoln, the signers of the Declaration of Independence are being renounced as traitors against Freedom. American patriotism and the "American Way" are no longer the way for a good portion of the population. I say this, not to take sides, but to illustrate how fickle Patriotic spirit, or any spirit, can be.

The preferred spirit for promoting spirituality would be an attitude of optimism and of confidence using intuition, creativity and subjective feelings to make sense out of reality. Rather than denigrate people long gone and not able to defend themselves, better to offer a solution that does not discriminate against still another group. We know where we should be going (that is, toward justice and fairness for all). Presently society eliminates injustice for one group by placing injustice toward another constituency. Rather than allowing the spirit of what the Germans call Zeitgeist or "The Spirit of the Age" to dictate what is fairness, seek to agree on a more stable reference point. Presently many attribute our reference point as being The Media or "The Powers That Be," which is anything but consistent; many, deep down, though maybe not even consciously, sense something is missing. Jesus used the term "The Poor in Sprit," (Matthew 5:3) as being a better determinant of justice. His assessment is what is missing is a stable, optimistic spirit or outlook held by the majority leading to an ideal world where no one, neither the poor nor rich are slighted. Jesus' position is that only with an "Ideal Person or God," one not playing favorites who could act as a source for unbiased treatment would such a world be possible. From a theological viewpoint Jesus pictured God as a real person, or in modern terms some would say "A Consciousness." But Jesus called him Father to put things in relatable, human terms. Very interestingly, Plato, a philosopher who was not religious, did the same. He pictured God as the ideal of all beautiful things, the epitome of all that is "good," all justice, kindness and loving. Plato then attempted to emulate that Ideal. From a strictly logical viewpoint, you the reader, are invited to pick one of these two optimistic positions to follow for meaning and purpose, whether religious or secularly oriented. The purpose of this session is to acquaint the reader with Spirituality. Though I find that combining both outlooks, secular and mystical, has an advantage, that is not what we are stressing here. A spiritual perspective, however one conceives the concept is always the most important first step, as far as I'm concerned.

The second verse I want you to consider is Matthew 16:26. Here Jesus again highlights the spiritual aspect of life. "What good will it be for a man if he gains the whole world, yet forfeits his soul?" Or what would a man exchange for his soul, his entire being? Jesus is contrasting the physical life of seeking only material treasures versus spiritual treasures and values. When laid out clearly, the choice is not really a difficult one, if we look at this the way Jesus outlined. A traveler can take the path leading to material wealth and physical assets or the path to higher values as the priority. At the end of a life, most of us would opt for the values in lieu of the material which are least enduring and easily tired of over time. Nothing wrong with owning a yacht but if we lose a close friendship, a devoted spouse or a close bond between parent and child over a physical possession, in the long run a loving bond is most enduring. Or which will give you more pleasure in the end, passing on that boat or passing on the memories with those you truly care for or whom you have cared about? Paraphrasing Jesus, "Is going through life feeling good about yourself and your memories where you were closely connected with friends and family worth the effort? Is it worth forfeiting the prospect of sharing never-to-be repeated-times with loved ones in exchange for spending those days working through vacation time to catch up at the office and maybe get ahead in the corporation?" Jesus is intimating in the SHORT-RUN the material may appear to be worth the price. However, in the LONG-RUN living a lifetime experiencing those spiritual rewards regularly and, in the end, being able to pass on the love and loyalty to those closest to us is definitely worth the price. Living spiritually means not allowing the media or peer pressure to dictate how one should think and what values one personally must aspire to. Spirituality means not forfeiting the non-material higher order values in one's personal life AND having the DREAM of seeing a just and fair world under the control of a beneficent, all-powerful force if one accepts the possibility of this mystical hope. Just because in some colleges such a belief is not currently fashionable does not make it an unreasonable dream, though it is not the professor's dreams. And just because those paying for your education insist on your living a life on their terms doesn't negate your terms. The sooner one starts to question the dictatorial commands of others, the sooner one senses he or she is truly living. Don't misunderstand what I'm advocating though. Based on my life experience, often what someone with more experience is suggesting to you may BE the best way. The purpose of your questioning another's input, is not just an exercise in insisting on choosing a different course, or proving we made our own choice. We choose so we are able to feel in control and can say, "I did what the HR department suggested but I was the one sensing it was the best choice for me personally. "

A little more about my background may help explain my position better. When I was fourteen the catalyst that started me to dream was becoming a Christian. I was forced to begin thinking about why I was here, in existence and whether I had a unique purpose all my own. I was choosing for myself, I felt in control, I was happy and satisfied. However, long about eighteen I condescended to do what those I looked up to thought was best for me (and they were not even my parents.) After a few years I realized, I had made the choice of career and lifestyle and I no longer had that feeling of excitement and anticipation. Sometime later, when I was age thirty, I realized and admitted to myself, "I am just not happy! I'm not satisfied with how my life is going. What is missing? What deep down is really missing?" It became perfectly clear then I had made mistakes along the way. When planning for the future I had ignored taking into consideration that I was and am now a unique being. I had ignored including in my equation my personality, my capabilities and my true passion. Once I then consulted my wife and life-partner, along with my inner feelings (which is the spirituality portion of my being) I was able to see clearly where the true me was pushing me to go, almost forcing me to go. When I resolved and acted, I sensed a feeling of peace in knowing I had gained back my soul, my true being, again. I had not forfeited that valuable possession for something I had never chosen years before. From that point on, I started living first as a spiritual being and only secondarily as a physical creature. From this new position, I have always gauged the success in my life by "Life Satisfaction." And now after a lifetime I can admit even in times of tremendous turmoil there have only been a few days here and there when I did not feel deep life satisfaction. I'm not gloating or bragging, I'm giving all the credit to those individuals before me and a higher power that gave me insightful wisdom to employ their insights and the ideas I stumbled on myself. I can testify to the surpassing power of spirituality.

One of the main reasons I perceive why so often the average person does not employ this higher outlook is the tendency to try to understand the non-material from the material world as we experience it in our lives. Starting in ancient times, those attempting to explain the complex world of environmental nature and human nature fashioned their explanations from what they were familiar and comfortable with. One Logical assumption was that some kind of intelligence was the source of all creation and logically that intelligence must have human form since only humans had minds that could dream and conceive. These higher powers were perceived as anthropomorphic, being like humans. And not just in physical appearance but in intellectual and emotional capacity similar to mankind. Picturing God as an old man with a long white beard may not be so much a detriment to comprehending the non-material, but mentally this did create major problems. The Old Testament of the Bible started picturing the All-Powerful God as a man with flowing bejeweled robes of the finest material. Then, just like man, God must have human tendencies. There is love, forgiveness, compassion, all wonderful and beautiful. But then, what about jealousy, anger as humans know it, the tendency to pay back hurt? As time gone on in our modern world, seekers of truth have started thinking more "outside the box," more spiritually, as I refer to this method. Even the latter prophets of Old Testament fame began picturing God not just as a man but metaphorically as magnificent, dazzling lights, fire and rainbows (Ezekiel 1:25-8) or precious, shining jewels sparkling with myriads of colors in another passage. And now, with the world of quantum physics we are coming to find even all material objects are really composed of waves and energy. Furthermore, science still will have to create or crack the code of how to describe consciousness and intelligence, yet those physical quantum discoveries actually make it easier to conceive of what an All-Powerful God can be conceived as, certainly not a human person. However, we envision this God the vast majority of our world's population believes in a God and use the tools of spirituality in their every-day life. But what has forced many to abandon religion is the anthropomorphic and emotional picture of God painted by two thirds of the world religions. However, using simple reasoning, most adults can deduce that a God so far above the little "ants" we humans are in comparison, such a God has enough self-worth and self-esteem not to have any tendency to be bothered by petty issues as we humans. He, even now I catch himself using the human term "He" in reference to God, is far above any need for what we humans sense as "anger" and the need to get back at someone to retaliate for a personal afront against him. People now reason, the idea of God torturing someone for all eternity due to him living a lifetime of seventy or eighty years without reverence to Him seems over-kill. That does not make sense logically. What some religions taught in the past was not complimentary to what we might call the "Eternal Consciousness" for want of a better term. I do want to apologize to many of my follow Christian friends who still accept the old-time description of an angry, vindictive God. Many of you are spiritual persons, in spite of how you were raised to believe. Now, at least, be realistic enough to admit, "I don't have all the answers myself. "The Bible talks of punishment for selfish living, which makes sense, but could it be that punishment is brought upon us rather than by God to punish out of anger? At least, think about that possibility.

Since my study here is for the benefit of all seekers of truth (truth, simply meaning reality as observed by an unbiased source). I hope we can see why members are leaving religious institutions. For one, many have never been taught to think spiritually. And, again, spirituality is simply taking time from our busy day-to-day to stop and contemplate, "Why is it my gut tells me there is something larger and greater than just me? I've had those experiences, when by chance good things happen to me. How do I get more of those type of events? There has got to be a way for me to protect my loved ones and me from the evil permeating this world, but how?" When one thinks like that, that's spirituality and the optimism of spirituality allows us to feel answers are out there for the searching.

I am not sure I made it clear what I keep repeating in this volume. The thesis here is when a person learns the basic principles of living his or her life will invariably improve. That stands to reason, doesn't it? If one can avoid putting himself in circumstances that engender difficulties, he avoids the negative consequences. Furthermore, most of the principles of spirituality are ones we already know from our own experience of living. For instance, we should know, the worst habit we can get into is believing the lies we tell ourselves. When we keep repeating, "I'm so stupid. I always make mistakes like this!" Studies prove we will subconsciously do what we tell ourselves and believe what we tell ourselves. These thoughts become Self-Fulfilling Prophecies. You will read more about this in another section of this book. Further psychology is discovering the power of love even when we have to force ourselves to learn to love and think of others' welfare in conjunction with our own; good things come back to us science demonstrates. More on this elsewhere. Along those lines I will also just mention Forgiveness. Studies in the last 20 years have shown that learning to forgive allows us to stop carrying extra baggage, hatred and vindictiveness, around with us. We could be using that energy dissipated needlessly on far more productive activity.

I am not going to enumerate, one by one, the other principles of spiritual living here. With an open mind, our own experiences in living make them quite clear. The fact that most religions have discovered the same principles independently is an indication of the work of spirituality. For example, the last five of the biblical Ten Commandments are also enumerated in Buddhist scripture completely independent from Judeo/Christian thought. One of the praiseworthy aspects of religion is the practice of formulating the best practical ways to live life. Even the secular philosophers of old, like the classical Greeks, prepared a list of virtues, attitudes and practices as guidelines for successful living. A spiritual person will reason, why is it that these gems of thought keep popping up independently throughout history and throughout the world? The reason is they work! As people become more spiritually aware they consciously come to desire to live a certain way, not because God or a king dictated how to live but because the spiritual way is the best way to live. I look back and reflect, why is it I don't have any enemies I know of? Why is it I could be married to the same woman for over fifty years and still have her as my best friend by my side? Why is it I don't have any estranged kids? Why is it I'm comfortable financially? Why is it I sleep so soundly every night? I know the answers, they have very little to do with my capabilities and less to do with life circumstances. Mostly they have to do with how I learned to live and when I made a wrong move, I was quick to learn from my mistakes. I was honest with myself. I learned to say, "Well, I made a mistake. I did it out of ignorance; I won't do that again." That is spiritual thinking and that is what I am attempting to teach.

The point I am making is not to convert you to Christianity. My purpose here is to teach you spiritual living. Once you start to live that way it becomes a way of life with amazing outcomes. From my experience, I would like to see you as a Christian, not a religious Christian but a spiritual Christian. My searching has led me to that path and a fantastic life. But I am not going to presume I have all the answers. I am only speaking from my own exploration and experience. My modus operandi is to accept ideas that really work, wherever the source of those ideas. Interestingly, most of these ideas of Christianity are taught in some form in most religions. Even countries that are no longer Christian, still live by virtue of their historical Christian background and heritage and that is why they are renowned for their quality of life. I have in mind countries like Sweden, Denmark, Norway and others. Those countries still revere the virtues of love, justice, kindness, forgiveness, compassion, peace and many more first taught them by Christianity and espoused to a degree beyond that of other overtly Christian countries. Those Scandinavian countries practice peace, justice, and forgiveness to an exemplary extent.

Throughout this book I have and will highlight some of the spiritual insights from Christianity because I have studied its philosophy extensively. I can assure you if you live by these principles your life will be enhanced and will flourish whatever else you do. My assurance is valid since I have lived it. And as I have intimated, spiritual ideas may at first appear illogical but when stripped of prejudice will always prove accurate. For example, the Bible repeats the phrase, "When I am weak then I am strong." That may not make sense on the surface but once laid out and approached with an open mind it becomes very clear. I mentioned this phrase previously. I dwell on it often since it is at the crux of spirituality. The phrase goes back some two thousand years. I would never have discovered this most powerful of ideas on my own, I was taught by other thinkers before me who passed it on. Fortunately, I was always open to new ideas. When it was suggested, I read (2 Corinthians 12:10). The words (as mentioned before), "When I am weak then I am strong," I could not help but be intrigued since the words appeared to contradict themselves. But I forced myself to think the reasoning through. Then later, in an instance, it became perfectly clear. When I was weak, either physically or mainly emotionally, I have acknowledged my state of mind and immediately this phrase came to consciousness. I noted that when I was weak, like in that moment, I was forced to rely on others, those with more experience, or had to stop and contemplate my options. I discovered there are often literally limitless possibilities out there. As long as I am optimistic and recognize the flow of benevolence present in the universe, it is as if a spirit of possibilities is waiting for me to latch on to any one of them. Good things happen. This is the way I am led to think about our human predicament. I tend to think along the lines of one of the first writers who helped revitalize Jewish theology. He put it this way at 2 Timothy 2:13, "If we are FAITH-LESS he remains FAITH-FUL, for he cannot disown himself." This tells me that others have sensed as I have that all creation is part of God. We are part of God and, as the writer here reasons, God cannot disown himself. He cares for himself and those who are part of Him. Everything we need to survive is out there in the world for our benefit. There is no way I can prove that to you, you must try it and prove it to yourself. As the verse notes, being faith-less is the normal state of most of us. In our times many, perhaps most, never are taught to think spiritually when we were young. Going to church when young, where you may have been able to learn the rudiments of optimism, is no longer a tradition and secular schooling never was intended to teach faith beyond faith in one's government or faith in oneself. Young people especially are desperately in need of something to believe in, something with a sense of certainty. The percent of atheists in our US society has been relatively constant (about 4%), for a number of generations now (Pew Survey, 2019). Even the number of agnostics, those who do not know what to believe has remained constant at approximately 4%. Yet by inference, the number of spiritual seekers has remained relatively constant though less religious. The possible reason is, as we have noted, we are all part of God. God is in our DNA; we sense an automatic affinity for one another. We all have the same heritage, and we all came from the same place, same eternal circumstances, the same consciousness that existed long before the Big Bang that created the physical world. We are destined to continue to sense that "nudge" toward the spirit of family and relationship and sense of feeling part of something greater and more powerful than ourselves. Many of us have lost touch with our connection with mankind and with God. Yet, we are so close. Can you muster the fortitude to admit "I do not have all the answers and I am not afraid to be open to new ideas?"

However, most of what we will discuss in this volume will be of a spiritual nature, using our boundless imagination and not religious rules. We will talk about these principles in several other chapters. Furthermore, a corresponding thesis is that a humans' first concern is to cultivate the habit of spiritual thinking and then, if and when they are ready, decide if religion can enhance one's outlook. When you finish this book, you will look at life in a whole different way, if you have not already discovered the concept. If you have already come to these conclusions, you will be saying "My outlook has been transformed to being positive, optimistic and ever searching." Welcome to the journey.

Chapter 2

First Half Life Seasons

Nature teaches us that our world consists of SEASONS; we notice seasons in weather, seasons with plants and animals and even humans. Unfortunately, it took me years before I truly appreciated the beauty of "Life Seasons" we humans experience. I understand now how critical it is we learn the lessons of SEASONS since this phenomenon will answer many of life's questions and concerns about meaning, purpose, direction and much more.

This is my thesis. Recognizing the seasons we go through in life is critical and living consciously in each season of life is vital. Furthermore, anxiously rushing through a life season without learning while living in that time period is a dreadful mistake. One can miss the insights to be learned from each life season and then there is the fear of missing an indispensable lesson necessary for a flourishing and complete life. This session is about the first season of life, in many respects and arguably the most important, if we are to start out on the right track.

While growing up, I was blessed to have been born in a part of the world where there were four distinct seasons. Looking back to when I was age fifteen, I couldn't choose which I liked better, even the cold blowing winters brought the excitement of sledding and ice skating. There was always a pond close by or public park to walk to whenever we kids felt like winter sports. Then in the summer we'd go to the local parks to pick teams for sandlot baseball. In a sense back then there were no seasons. Winter transitioned into Spring, then into Summer. Always fun things to look forward to. Then as I got older, I got married and had children and the beautiful rhythm started all over again. Looking forward to a snowy day to go sledding with the Kids, then looking forward to summer on the beach. Life was one lyrical musical piece with the periodic motif reappearing throughout. Living in Michigan all my life was perfect. Friends would excitedly exclaim about going to Florida for two weeks during the winter and I'd retort, "In a few months it will be summer here, why not enjoy the warmth of a home and fireplace while we wait?" Then long about the time I hit my fifties and after ten days of single digit or sub-zero Fahrenheit weather I finally thought it might be nice to go to Florida for a winter break. Never been before, never cared to, but that year I decided to go and have ever since. It was then that I started to appreciate the climate changing seasons. And not long after, I recognized there was also such a thing as seasons in a human life course, our seventy to ninety years. I don't know if it was that I was enjoying myself so much that seasons didn't register. Now that I'm in my last portion of my Second Half, I am able to pass on what I have learned. I know you'll find it insightful. Perhaps it might have been nice to have learned the lesson about seasons earlier, but in reality, I had to learn from experience.

I write this paper especially addressed to those who have some experience with the SPIRITUAL SIDE of life. What I mean by that is understanding that human minds are limited in their capacity to comprehend. In addition to a rational mind, humans have such capabilities as intuition, feelings and emotions that work at the sub-conscious level. Spirituality means a person does not arbitrarily dis-count the possibility of a non-physical dimension that could impinge on our physical world. Similarly, my paper is addressing those who are Christians or are willing to look at life with an open mind. Christianity starts with several simple premises that are logical but cannot be proved totally, no different than science, which starts with several simple premises that cannot be proved either. In either case starting with those few premises and proceeding logically and follow-ing what one learns from experience one can come to conclusions that make sense and explain so much more in life. I have found, having the benefit of both methods (Mind and Heart) provides maximum understanding of life. I will use Bible verses occasionally for those who are Christians but the principles of living we discuss are easily followed by non-Christians and the result is a system that explains without contradiction so much of life whether the seeker is Christian or not, religious or not. So why take the time to read this short lesson in living? Life stories are a dime a dozen. You're going to get this guy telling you of his three marriages and what went wrong or you'll get the gal to brag about her idyllic life with a perfect marriage and with-out a worry about finances. But be realistic. I come along, claiming I've had a meaningful, fulfilling, flourishing life but had to endure deaths, of my own son among them, lost jobs, near death experiences all without regrets. The difference in my case from other coaches is early on I found a path, a way of life, a philosophy that really works. Other will relate what they learned from their mistakes, what not to do, I'll provide advice on what does work, what does lead to a flour-ishing, fulfilling life with minimal regret. Another thing I have going for me is I was born a philosopher. As much as I wanted to be a pro football player at age twelve soon realized I didn't have the physical build or the level of athletic talent required. I learned to be content being the thinker, the analyst I am. I have always had to test ideas out logically but also pragmatically; does it really work? The other good fortune I had was to be introduced to the Christian philosophy at a young age. I don't mean the extreme fundamentalist type where most ideas in the Bible are taken literally or the extreme liberal type where values were of secondary concern. I learned early on Jesus' simple message with its optimistic view of life and the expectation of more good than bad in life, if and when one looks for it. Love energizes and makes the world go around. And because there had to be something that initiated the Big Bang that formed the uni-verse, we can call that something "God." With that starting point we build the foundation of all truth, all meaning, all desire from a finite beginning. And all one has to do is use those simple principles Jesus taught to build a life that offers hope, love, satisfaction, meaning and flourishing over time. I don't claim to have all the answers, no human does. Our human minds are so limited and finite it would be impos-sible to grasp the complexity of the infinite universe by approaching it from a strictly finite mind.

My study here is going to apply specifically to what we can learn in the FIRST Half of Life. Probably the best way to present this is to first contrast the First Half of Life to the Second Half. Some twenty-five years ago I wrote a comprehensive study of life's First Half. That study was written after I had lived some twenty-five years in the first half as an adult, analyzing what I observed and what others learned from research and experimentation. With that study

I presented eight areas of life that needed to be negotiated for a balanced full life. My book, FINDING FULLFILLMENT (Vision Books, 1995) presented the "Eight F's" I learned or discovered, was taught or had experienced that made that first half of life so empowering, exciting, meaningful and fulfilling for me. Many principles I learned for life's First Half apply equally as well to my Second Half; But the First Half is when we initially explore these ideas.

CONTRASTS

I find the simplest way to explain Life Seasons, two of them being the First Half and Second Half is to start with the contrasts between the two. Many writers like to use the model of two halves like in an American football game. I prefer the idea of three main seasons in life, young adult, mature adult and senior member of society with that middle season a transition from one aspect to another. I discuss that in another article. Using the analogy of two halves in a football game, winning in the first half does not mean winning the game. And losing in the first half rarely predicts who will win when the game is over. Life's First Half, as I showed in my first book, put the emphasis on a person's finding out who he or she is as a person and learning to like himself or herself. As all of you know, those who have already lived a good part of that first half, there is an awful lot to comprehend in the initial half. A person is required to become educated intellectually. mentally, emotionally and socially. You, as a unique individual, are given the task of choosing a career, one that will provide the financial wherewithal to allow you to live without being a burden on others unless you have a serious disability. Further, I discovered most individuals even with physical handicaps find the strength and determination to provide for themselves if they are encouraged and assisted to do so. Next, a young person confronts the necessity of finding a set of friends to travel through life's journey with. Sooner or later, if that young person is fortunate, she will find a lifetime partner to share the journey and, if chosen well, will have found a best friend. That is a lot to accomplish in one's First Half of existence. Starting out with a set of potentials to finally becoming a mature adult capable of navigating a lifetime journey is a tremendous task. Just think, when you were a teen, you started out disliking, perhaps hating yourself, hating your looks, hating your parents, hating being forced into schooling you felt was irrelevant. Through all of these ordeals you finally begin to start liking yourself! You gain competence in living, you become proficient in a job. You eventually have children, start to mature, and as expected you become competent mentally, emotionally, socially and, if fortunate, able to comprehend the value of a spiritual grounding.

With so much required to accomplish, all centered on constructing and crafting a self, is it any wonder you have had to acquire a self-centered mindset? You had to think of self foremost, you were forced to and expected to. Realize there was nothing wrong with that. You were required to think of self first or your shared human assignment would never have been completed. Sure, that is selfishness but that is all part of life's first half. If you navigated it well you emerged a competent adult. If you've ever thought it through for yourself, you realize your First Half of life is reserved to make you a productive member of society, fending for yourself and doing your part to share responsibility with others to make your community and your circle, a better place because of your presence there. How long does it take to fulfill that assignment? How long does it take to get to the point where you like yourself? When will you feel you fit in with your peers and feel you have something to contribute to your friends, to your community and to society? Unfortunately, some never get to that point!

Given that there are so many major projects packed into the first half of a life course and all are related to one's identity, it would be difficult not to think selfishly about oneself during that period. Thinking about self is a necessity, something God expects of us. Don't feel ashamed, we all go through the same process. The problem is when you ONLY think about self to the exclusion of others including your Maker. Here is where balance enters the picture. In fact, this is why my book on navigating life's first half stresses the virtue of a balanced life. That was the major thesis of my study. I isolated eight life areas to be cognizant of while building one's identity. For example, our identity includes our FAMILY, from whence we came, our FRIENDS, those to whom we relate, our FINANCES or career we chose to provide resources for sustenance, the importance we place on FITNESS, including physical, mental, emotional fitness and then, of course, our level of FAITH, our picture of the mysterious, larger picture of attempting to identify truth, reality, meaning, all the most important requisites of personal identity. Then come requisite ingredients of FAME, FORTUNE and FACULTIES that we'll touch on later in our discussion. I have found many Christians have been taught it is selfish and sinful to worry about self-identity and self-esteem. Actually, just the opposite is true. Remember Jesus teaches us "To love our neighbor as ourself." If we don't LOVE OURSELVES, don't have a level of pride and sense of well-being about ourselves, how can we truly love our neighbor, our friend, our family as we are supposed to love ourselves? Is it sinful to want the very best for our family, for our children? Shouldn't they, too, be given priority time from us to nurture their security and well-being? Shouldn't we as parents desire the financial wherewithal to offer options for our children's education or medical attention? Kind of selfish, isn't it? But that's what makes good parents, that desire for our family's best interest. All selfish, selfish, selfish. But that's where balance comes into play. As I've come to know God, there is no question He wants these things for all of us. He makes provision so societies inherently have resources for those necessities, though not always as readily available due to human selfish intervention.

The important thing to realize is all this essential, self-centered work has to be completed by the time one is able to fully give attention to life's SECOND HALF! Ideally, during the first, all self-centered, self-building, self-esteeming elements will be completed to a level where we can begin giving greater attention to our legacy leading into the future. If we haven't gotten to the point of liking ourself, being grateful for our attributions and our well-being, how can we truly work fully on Jesus' directive to love our neighbor as ourselves? Yes, the first half may perhaps require that we spend more time preparing self and loving self-more than neighbor. But in the second half, we are able to devote more time looking after the unselfish interests and well-being of others. We will always be working on our virtues and our capabilities. But to the extent we've made progress growing to maturity mentally (wisdom), emotionally (self-control), and spiritually (knowing our place in the scheme of things), we are able to seek new, higher levels of service to fellow man.

So here we are, in review, the First Half of life is building our ego, building our capabilities, and competencies while in the Second Half a conscious effort is necessary to let go of self and ego. We built those parts of our being up but now's the time to put them aside. So much of the First Half was devoted to taking PERSONAL RESPONSIBILTY and building CONFIDENCE and our ABILITIES, thinking about ME, I, MY welfare. Then comes the time to make a conscious effort to START GIVING BACK. Once we gain maturity and once we have gained experience and the confidence that comes with experience, we are in a position to truly help others as they have helped us in our SEASON of building. Once we start liking ourselves, we feel far less pressure to prove ourselves and less pressure to compete and scrape out our way to the top. In many cases we feel satisfied with what we've accomplished or at least realized we've probably gotten to the station of life where we conclude exerting ourselves to move a little higher in stature is probably not worth the effort. And especially if we like ourselves there is no need to have to prove anything to anyone, least of all to ourselves. We've proved to ourselves we are as important and as resourceful as the average guy or gal, or maybe a little better (we think). Now's the time to start reaping the benefits of our hard work. The main benefit, I think, is the valuable TIME to do what we're meant to do. This is the ideal situation. As you have no doubt noticed, some NEVER attain this desired level of understanding, never satisfied, never feeling good about self. Maybe never got the education he sought, never found the right partner she sought, never got the exciting job he sought. If it's you we're talking about, fill in the blank, "I never got..." Hopefully such a person will stop and admit, "Enough is enough. Yes, I made mistakes but I'm not going to waste the rest of my life crying about that missing element. I must be realistic."

Being realistic also means admitting maturity takes time. A Christian doesn't become a mature Christian with chronological years. There is a world of difference in one's confidence, understanding of life, personal meaning once an individual has had years of exposure and living as a Christian. It takes only a moment to become a Christian. Simply admitting to an unhappy existence, asking for divine help and accepting Jesus' offer of Salvation can be accomplished in one sitting. The experience part takes years. Getting one's life in order and making decisions on the self-centered issues of life, career, making friends, liking family, ordering financial resources all take time. Some of us have to work on these several times over to get it right. I didn't ever think about a career till I was thirty. Then it took me several tries to do it successfully. But the partner part came easily in my case. The first girl I enjoyed being with and not just infatuated with turned out to be my best friend. The education part took me till forty-five or fifty. The part about not worrying about what others thought of me or about me took me even longer. We keep trying and then once we find it or have it, we start perfecting it. With my marriage, we're down to only two things that we disagree about and still haven't gotten those resolved fully yet. Fortunately, we didn't have to agonize over whether we should have children. The first one came along long before we wanted to make any decisions on such major questions. From personal experience and life-long obser-vation, I've found very rarely does a person ever feel he has enough life experience under his belt to feel he has the level of competence and confidence to convince himself he has attained the stature desig-nated "mature." The exception is possibly someone sixteen to twen-ty-one years of age, they might think they have nothing left to learn but that sensation soon is lost. Similarly, often a person may be in her fifties before she senses within the feeling of having walked long enough with God and self that she's ready for any eventuality that life directs her way.

Some of the guidelines I suggest a Christian use to gauge his or her level of maturity could be the included items in a checklist I'll offer later. But another way of gauging this, is to ask, "Am I clear as to who I am, do I know myself, my capabilities and my defi-ciencies?"(Yes, knowing them, not necessarily having perfected or eliminated them, that's a lifetime task.) Also, do I feel a certain sense of security yet? Total security is never a possibility in this life. But like financial security, you never can preclude the inevitability of another world economic failure and Great Depression where at least 25% of the work force is without a job and without government subsidies. But you can get to the point where you have no debt and you have an emergency fund of cash for unforeseen eventualities. That is a minimum measure of security, at least. By the same token, living in security means having done one's homework including forgiving others for their improprieties toward us, having asked forgiveness from those we have hurt. Even sensing that God realizes we are trying is so important. Critical is having friends, family, church who we know care for us, about us. Once we have those, we have a modicum of security. Also, in the last twenty years a brand-new issue of identity has arisen, one that seldom used to arise. That's the question of sexuality or gender identity. This is not the place or time to explore the ramifications here but be apprised that you or someone you know may still be wrestling with their sexuality or especially their gender, to the extent they feel the need to prove their worth and capability and feel distrust and hatred toward those one perceives as having an unfair advantage over them. Many men now have to deal with a changing world where physical strength was once the "trump card" to get your way. And many women feel their capabilities cannot off set the fact they are not a part of the "old boy network." So much more could be said that puts both men and women at a disadvantage in the new social world we find ourselves in. Nevertheless, we all must put to rest these nagging perceived disadvantages before one can truly devote oneself to the assignments of life's Second Half.

A distinguishing idea in Christianity is the thought that it is incumbent on us to keep growing. The Bible encourages us to grow to maturity. Hebrews 6:1 asserts. "moving forward, not laying again a foundation." This pertains to a number of ways a believer will "move forward." Becoming mature gives the connotation of growing to one's full potential. Just as a child is expected to grow to physical maturity, to his expected physical stature so a community expects that its members grow to maturity mentally, emotionally and socially. Spending a short time talking to a person makes it quite clear if that person has accomplished those tasks yet. And as we have already noted, our society has devolved to the point where an appreciable number of young people are stuck at the level of adolescence well into age thirty. Kids, if we should still call them kids at that age, are not prepared financially and emotionally to leave home as adults. They are still living with mom and dad, enjoying a carefree life of leisure. Back when the agricultural society was the norm, kids at five or six years old had their chores of work in the chicken coop or corn-fields. Can we call the expectations in our modern society progress? Even when I was young, a boy of eighteen, whether graduated from high school or not was expected to be working full time or be in college (back then only twenty percent of students went on to college).

You know when you think about it, it's kind of a paradox. When children are no longer infants and begin to talk, they can be the most delightful of characters. Interestingly, they tend to start out showing signs of being spiritual creatures. I take my grandson, Peter, here as an example. At six years old I am amazed at his ingenuity. His insights about life are way above his years. That's the beginning of a spiritual mind. It's a delight to hear his fresh responses to what to adults are minor, mundane occurrences. He's transfixed when he watches a video about bees or insects and how they go about their business making honey or gathering food for the little community. I almost feel embarrassed that I don't feel the spark of wonder in my eyes that he has in his. I can sense that his response to new experiences is what is intended for all of us. And what imagination little kids have. They look at things outside the normal connotation. That, again, is one sign of being spiritually minded, the understanding of how special life can be. The Spiritual plane includes Originality and Creativity, along with Inspiration. Inspiration or "inspirit" is another factor in a spiritual outlook. I am reminded when I look at little children that we were made that way.

Living in conjunction with seasons forces one to keep in sight one's personal life purpose and to integrate all activities into a clear, manageable bundle. Recognizing you do not have to do it all in life's first half teaches you patience and relieves an awful lot of stress. I can vouch for the fact that elimination of excess worry and anxiety and increased joy and satisfaction follows with welcoming and enjoying each changing season. Now, it's your turn. Where are you in your life journey? You want to be in a position to discern what habit or virtue needs to be perfected next. To the extent you're diligent, a flourishing life is ahead.

LIFE-COURSE SURVEY

This survey will get you to thinking about how your life is progressing. We encourage you to analyze all aspects of your life. At this point, simply answer each question honestly for yourself. Then hold on to this document for future reference. No one else will see this but you.

Mark each as: Very True VT), Somewhat True (ST), Neutral (N), Somewhat false (SF), False (F)

____On the surface, my life is going well.

____My physical health does not prevent me from doing all I wish to do.

____Mentally and emotionally I feel strong.

____I don't have much stress in my life now.

____I have a close knit family in my home with little fighting and bickering.

____I am happy with my extended family, we get together often with little friction.

____I have enough time to do most of the activities I wish to do each week.

____I am happy with the time I take for relaxation, recreations and vacations yearly.

____I am quite satisfied with my career or retirement status.

____I enjoy working where I do and with my colleagues and my responsibilities etc.

____Financially I have the funds needed for a comfortable life.

____I am saving or have saved enough funds to get me through retirement.

____I have several close friends.

____I have good number of friends and family with whom to do things.

____I consider myself a spiritual person.

___I have found a religious organization with whom I enjoy fellowship.

___I consider myself a charitable person.

___I feel I am a valuable member of my community.

___I have found satisfying answers to most of the life questions I've asked.

___I feel my life has meaning and purpose now.

___I like myself and who I have become up to this point in my life.

___List the traumatic events you have experienced through your life, such things as loss of a close friend or loved one, a serious accident, loss of a job, divorce or emotional upheaval, etc.

Pay particular attention to any statement marked, "false" or "somewhat false," Which?

Then ask which traumatic events still affect you now?

Anything else that you feel needs to be discussed?

Don't be discouraged, everyone starts out with a number of areas he or she realizes are concerns. As long as we have isolated what are major concerns, you can work on them!

Chapter 3

A God Paradigm

One problem today is the paradigm of God we may have inherited. With the prominence of Post-Modern Philosophy and modern scientific discoveries, the term "god" requires reassessment for some. Through upbringing, school, past culture we've inherited a picture of God handed down over thousands of years. This is not the time to expand on my thesis that everyone needs a "god" of some sort, regardless of how they might consider that entity. I'm only going to offer some ideas on updating our concept of 'god.' When we talk of a "god," we all mean by that term something more profound than ourselves. Something more powerful, wiser and more transcendent in time and space. How one puts those elements in one package is a matter of diversity of thought. Some have conceived of their god being simply nature or a part of nature. Others found it easier to use what they knew and could relate to, a human form. The Greeks and Romans conceived of "gods" as "super" human, that's all. A person much like any human with all the foibles and imperfections but merely having superhuman powers. Only so many concepts of gods have survived as workable and useful though. We need not have all the answers for how and why these concepts are useful but they work and have survived the test of time. For hundreds of years we did not understand electricity, but we used the discovery to improve society as a result. The concept of "god" though not fully understood has helped millions of people cope with and direct their lives. My thesis (without the intention of presenting details here), is that most humans have a belief in something greater than themselves. And these diverse concepts help us to navigate through our lives.

We're now living in an era when, I believe, it's prudent and effective to ask ourselves what we mean by "god" and admit to ourselves who or what is our personal 'god.' The first question to ask is this, up to this point and based on how I live, what is the most powerful or most important force I personally trust? To some that's a person (e.g., a family head), a society (e.g., a communist or socialist government), self (an atheistic notion), scientific exploration or a traditional god. The majority of individuals admit they don't trust completely or fully any of these sources. Living in a changing, unstable world many desire something more stable for trust. The idea of a transcending, all powerful, all wise and benevolent (benevolence-that's the great contribution of Christianity to religion) entity has helped and will help millions cope with uncertainty. Unfortunately, our concepts of this entity have not kept up with our broader understanding of our world today. For example, most people when asked to think for a moment, will admit their concept of God as a physical person is not congruent with the idea of someone omnipresent, being everywhere needed at any given time.

Here's an example of an entity that can be omnipresent, permeating all societies simultaneously. The idea of an omnipresent God is not so hard to phantom after all. The power and wisdom of a group working in unison to promote love, for example, is omnipresent and much more effective than any one person. Some might call that synergy by the term "god." Indeed, that concept is entailed in the concept of Nature and its mechanisms such as Evolution being more prescient than any individual. Those are possible ways of conceiving of a god. However, some are still content with the traditional concept of God that has survived and has worked well for thousands of years. However, others might feel, for themselves, a need to make the concept more clearly relevant.

Nature, as a concept of god, is helpful to some seekers, especially if they prefer the idea that all there is in the universe are physical forms and forces. I guess that idea may be fine as a starting point but I personally found it artificially limiting. Claiming, "That's all there is," is not the mentality that galvanized the great discoveries and great exploration of human endeavor up to this point in human history. "Nature only" is a very limiting concept as we will come to see. I personally need a more useful understanding for A GOD PARADIGM to work. I'm a sociologist by profession so I know that stats can be juggled to suit one's personal interpretation. Therefore, it's important to check the sources and especially the questions asked. The 2008 Barna study is one I consider to be an example of an unbiased study. Open-ended questions can be difficult to interpret and choice questions *require a good range of non-leading questions. The Barna study asked, "which comes* closest to your belief in God? Yes, I believe there is a God. (78% answered affirmatively), Not a God as such but a universal spirit or higher power. (15%), Neither of the above. (6%) and unsure. (1%) So in this study 6% of the population was truly atheistic. This study seems to intimate that many of those who call themselves agnostic are saying they perceive there to be a higher power or universe spirit that binds us together. Other studies ask for names but terms like "agnostic" are quite ambiguous. Other studies that use terms for beliefs show 6% of those surveyed claim to be atheists and 8% claim to be agnostic. This appears to purport that most agnostics actually believe in some sort of pervasive spirit. Another very telling piece of data from our research that couples political and religious viewpoints is what you find when you ask about conservative and liberal leanings. 12% of the population consider themselves very conservative. Many of them are extreme Fundamentalists that consider the Bible to be read literally with little room for reasoning. On the other extreme 10% of the population consider themselves to be extremely liberal expecting society to have few if any restrictions on personal behavior regardless of the effect on fellow citizens. They also leave little room for negotiation with their demands. The vast majority (78%) are somewhere in the middle. This vast majority seems to be skewed somewhat to the more conservative side with most all Christian. Unfortunately, the media uses the term Christian to connote the extreme 12% of our society that make up only 15% of those purporting to be Christian as the definition of Christian while when talking of liberal never mentioning the 10% of extreme liberals (I'm talking of those 2 terms from a social more than political demarcation).

The other term that has appeared since the 1970's that seems to complicate our analysis is the term "spirituality." The term has a somewhat different connation but the majority now uses the term to denote belief in a higher power or a connectedness to the universe. We'll see that the majority of our population that considers themselves to be non-religious (that 15%) consider themselves to the "spiritual." Here is an example. A Newsweek poll of Americans in 2009 found that 60% of the surveyed said "Religion was very important to them while 78% claimed that "prayer was a very important part of their lives." It seems quite clear that the 18% (78-60) are individuals who are spiritual but non-religious while the vast majority of the religious groups are spiritual (but not all). So, while religion, as such, has diminished somewhat as a very important part of life, the slack has been taken up mostly by those who now consider themselves "spiritual" in nature.

My desire is to promote more dialog. And I'm heartened to see the data appears to support the fact that at least among those that call themselves agnostics there is a clear connection with those that call themselves Christian (the idea of spirituality). Even atheists I find would concede there is a synergy in the universe. What it is, how it works, let's hope we can unravel that in the future but most spiritual people are content to avail themselves to that source in the meantime. I would also expect that some atheists, that are atheists as a result of philosophical searching and religious questioning, might consider themselves spiritual in a sense. This idea of spirituality is again more specifically an American phenomenon some would say, part of our American culture, another step in the process of privatizing, personalizing or individualizing as we have been doing for 200 some years. A statement is being made that, "I don't need organized religion to live a life of faith and belief." So, the interpretation of our society becoming more secular is not backed up the data, leaving religion does not mean secular (devoid of reverence). This is borne out by studies of Millennials (those 18 to 29 or so). USA Today's study of Millennials in 2009 found that 65% of them were Christian, 8% of another religion, 14% had no religious preference, 8% agnostic and 6% atheist. That 14% with no preference we can infer are among those that admit to being spiritual. By the way, the study found of those who were believers, 50% claimed to go to a place of worship at least weekly.

FINDING YOUR TRUE SELF

Going a step further, pure logic comes to the conclusion that nothing can be proved true beyond doubt; that's the nature of nature. All reasoning starts with certain assumptions either stated or implied whether admitted or not. An atheist starts with the assumption that all knowledge and reasoning is a product of molecule and chemical reactions. So, the equipment of chemicals in the brain is the tool for apprehending knowledge. Can this be proved? Of course not. On the other hand, a Christian like me starts with the assumption there is intelligence from a source independent of the material. Can I prove it? Of course not. Let's not deny that's our current reality. The starting point of any discussion, I would conjecture would be to ask, "Are there any signs of intelligence in the universe (including us)?" I find many atheists will say yes, but not beyond the material world. A spiritual person, not necessarily a religious one will say yes too but will add, why needlessly bound your search to one plane only, if there are others?

The biggest problem I find with debate about belief in God is that belief in religion and belief in the non-material spiritual source are not the same. As we've seen from stats an appreciable number of people are not religious but are spiritual. So, to point to the failings of religion as the proof there is not a God is not logical. To debate whether religion is useful and to debate whether there is a God are two independent inquiries. To point to the failings of the Catholic Church, who for centuries was more political than religious, is irrelevant in the debate about whether there is a God. It's tantamount to claiming the corruption in the GOP is proof that Abe Lincoln, one of the early founders of the Republican Party was motivated by greed for power and wealth. Yet this is the main line of argument used by atheists.

Whether one is an atheist or not, most people would like to think there is a measure of justice in our world. However, there is only one belief system that supports that idea, belief in an all-powerful God. That's the conclusion Kant, the philosopher, came to. He admitted, "I believe in Justice, a righting of wrongs, belief in a God, a higher power, is the only logical conclusion." An atheist avows there is no truth (mainly because he can't prove there is such a thing) and since he believes all ideas can be reduced to chemical reactions there is no such thing as justice. If my inner spirit (whatever that is), soars to believe in truth, justice I cannot be an atheist since I would be hoping for something that I believe does not exist. So, if I want to entertain the possibility of justice, you've got but one choice, belief in God.

We can use the same sort of reasoning to see the consequence of believing in the scientific method of Reductionism to see it too leads to a dead end. On the other hand, belief in a higher power posits a light at the end of the tunnel, not a dead end. Reductionism is that idea that if you take apart any entity into its constituent parts one can better understand the makeup of that entity. The dead end I see in reductionism is the belief that all thinking and logic is based on chemical reactions, therefore I am admitting at the onset (or assuming) that my logic is limited to chemical reactions, and therefore, the mechanism I am using to examine life is limited indeed. I'm saying my admittedly limited (one size fits all logic) can only go so far. How do I know there isn't a superior logic not bound by the material chemicals? I can only see material if I only have and use a material magnifying glass. I admit, at the same time, I'm using a biased, imperfect method with results that must be biased AND IMPERFECT. I wish we could spend more time expanding the logic of this reasoning but this is not the venue to go into detail here.

Oh, by the way, reductionism leads to the conclusion there is no free will, just chemical reactions, not a pleasant thought but I can live with that. Fortunately, I don't have to, I can pretend to dream and who knows I might possibly find that dreams come true, I'll never know till I try. I can't try because I'm a reductionist and I only believe in the material. I think I'd rather go the less limiting route than the path of my atheist friend who says "what's the use of trying, there is no free will!" One more thing on reductionism... Animal studies keep coming up to the same dead end. Try as they may and I think it's laudable they try, animal behaviorists can teach animals (chimps in particular) the meaning of words, as many as 300 or so. That's astounding, but try as they may, they can't teach a nonmaterial thought. The words animals learn the meaning of are all material, house, food names even pain, maybe even a preliminary meaning of death that can be pointed to, but when it comes to concepts and ideas, there is a mental block. What about Meaning, Purpose, Justice, Truth (Oh, I'm sorry there is none) but what about future and, dare I say it, love? At some point in evolution there is this monumental jump from material to what I consider non-material. Now it may be possible that science will break the consciousness code and break the idea code. But what it does not prove, the believer in such things as dreams (free will) and justice (which seems to be illusory) and God (meaning something greater than chemicals) will say, "It's nice to know how this phenomenon works but my mind still tells me the amazement of life has a nonmaterial source you're not equipped to detect with your rudimentary material instruments."

Finally note that all atheistic arguments are one of 3 sorts. Please tell me if I'm wrong. Argument #1, Since people who purport to believe in God act unethically at times their contradictory actions must prove they must be wrong, ergo no God. Similarly, the Catholic

Church's hypocrisy proves there is no God. Ditto, Islam's horrible bloodshed over centuries proves there is no God. Huh, that does not make sense does it?...Argument #2 all arguments that claim to prove a God cannot be proved beyond doubt. Huh, what argument proves there is no God, of course, none. It's much easier to pounce on an argument than to come up with original ideas, cannot non-believers admit they have no proofs either? At least the Christian is honest and will say, "it's true, a little bit of faith is needed." I'd feel so much better if my atheist friend just admits the same thing, that a bit of faith is required whatever you believe, but I guess that's a dirty word, "FAITH."

Argument #3 One day, we're getting closer every day, then we'll crack the secret of life and consciousness, then what will you say? (Scare tactic, like the Hell tactic) but, Huh, what does that prove about whether there is or isn't a God? Oh, and argument #4, Christians are afraid to examine what science can prove and are willing to accept only what they are comfortable with. But come on now, there are hundreds of thousands of scientists that are Christian and do believe. Admittedly many Christians continue with what they are comfortable with, but most atheists are just as comfortable, especially comfortable with being free (not free will, of course, but at least seemingly free to live without responsibility) and when asked for their proof they resort to pointing to the crimes of religion which of course proves religion is not always ethical but has nothing to do with whether there is a God. Such reasoning does not even attempt to give a LOGICAL REASON FOR THEIR OWN BELIEF.

Interestingly the Bible never bothers to try to prove whether there is a God. Basically, it uses only two appeals to get the reader to think on a higher plane. The first is the idea that creation by a higher intelligence is self-evident. The writers saw no need to dwell on a proof since they assumed most reasonable people realized the beauty, the order, the design in nature was enough of a proof to them. Most Christians today are swayed by the argument for intelligent design. And as many as 80% from my informal studies agree with the basic concepts of evolution with the proviso of intelligent design. The state of nature around us is no absolute proof of a God's existence; it's only a fair indication. I, as a Christian, haven't gotten to the point of being able to put faith in something other than an intelligence. Science finds only a minimum amount of order can come from randomness. Pure Evolutionists must posit that in the beginning the potential for the material world must have existed with the potential for what appears at least to be intelligence. Can they go so far as to call that God?

The Bible uses symbols to describe God and unfortunately those symbols are taken literally by critics to claim contradicts. God is symbolized as one with a lion's power, an eagle's wide view, and the majesty of sparkling polished gems. A man of authority in long robes, an ancient white bearded man with the wisdom of the ages and even more recently in books like the Shack that picture him as a rotund black woman with infinite compassion and other times as a "Father knows Best" figure. I picture an energy flowing, surging in everything, flashing and pulsing in all matter and beyond. As an atheist I would not be prepared to give up the possibility of absolute truth, real meaning in life, connectedness to all on a super-material basis and communion with a higher power, all that can't be proved but missing to an atheist.

The First and standard proof of God is nature itself. To some that does not appear to be enough of a proof. While most observers have no difficulty analyzing the complexities of nature and conclude there is a fantastic design in nature. Based on the fact that the more complex human inventions become it is apparent the design proves an intelligence is behind them. To some, atheists , for example, that is a subjective conclusion. I'd have to respond, "yes, it is." However, I would have to remind my friends who are atheists that their conclusion is also very subjective. To claim non-intelligent Evolution is the only possible source of complexity is an extremely subjective and stubborn conclusion. Is there any reason Evolution and Intelligent Design cannot both be true? No, so why be so stubborn to not be open to that possibility?

So, I am hopeful, though, that intelligent design is a good starting point for dialog. This concept might be a good point of compromise. We can agree that life has evolved and we can see signs of fantastic, awe inspiring design. There are signs of intelligence in the Universe. Do I call this intelligence God and personify it or call it potential energy that toils to continue advancing? I have friends who espouse both viewpoints and we get along famously. To me, "intelligence" or "potential energy" are an adequate starting point in identifying what this God is that I believe in. I can't force anyone to take the step, that spiritual step or philosopher's step to personify God for use purposes only . One needs to prove for herself that she is more than chemical reactions and seek to break through the bounds that materialism artificially holds her in.

The second proof given in the Bible is what the Swedish philosopher Kierkegaard called "the Leap of Faith." Jesus gave the invitation, saying in effect, "I can't prove it to you in any other way but this. If you're tired, bored, feel burdened, unfulfilled, afraid and anxious, just try my solution which is based on a belief in God. You won't know till you try. The only way you'll know for sure is to try. That's what K called the Leap of Faith. Just pretend for a couple weeks you're part of something greater. You're no less valuable then all humans around you. You Deserve **Happiness As Much As The Next Person. You can connect to a source of power you haven't felt** before. Live as if you can't fail. Suspend judgment and work on believing like a little child would. See what happens. No one can dissuade you personally then. No one can claim, "You really didn't feel that serenity or that calmness or that inspiration or that surge of energy." You felt it; someone else can't argue with you that you didn't. Millions, who have done just that, can testify that it's true; no one can take that experience away from them. At least it's reality to them, its truth to them, and isn't that what an atheist believes, truth is reality? All an atheist can say is, "I've never felt that." But that is no indication that others have not. Millions have never felt in the zone, as the expression goes. If you aren't an athlete, a writer, painter or some creative person you may not have. But that doesn't disprove the experiences of these. Who would be foolish enough to say, it's just your imagination, there is no such thing. So if an individual can't bring himself to look at nature around her and agree there might be design or she can bring herself to just dream that she could be a part of something greater than her and want to have that feeling of being in the zone, so to speak, there's nothing more to say at this point.

This possibility opens the door to considering another liberating possibility many have not availed themselves of. I'm talking here about "inspiration." Don't be summarily turned off by that word, I'm using it very deliberately. Our world, nature, our planet is a living organism." Synergy," for want of a better word, has nurtured life to survive and progress. That force is at work in and through all of us. Sir Isaac Newton, arguably the greatest of scientists, informs us it was an apple falling that inspired him to comprehend the laws of gravity. In other words, nature "told" him about gravity. Inspiration just came. How that happens is another study, but he admits to being "inspired" to see the facts already bound up in natural elements, they were revealed or unlocked to him. Some of us are willing to accept inspiration in the physical sciences but not willing to admit inspiration in social settings, moral settings or meaning for existence. A double standard? Part of the problem I think, is that human life is more complicated than pure physical science. There are so many more variables intertwined in life. In science, one person can describe and conduct an experiment. Then another scientist can conduct the same experiment and will come up with identical results. However, you can't always duplicate a human life study. Psychologists run experiments on their college students under artificial conditions and wonder why another psychologist can't verify those results or may interpret them differently. Similarly, because of their cultural background, a society may accept a certain paradigm without question or proof it is the best course. A good example is the statistical data on identical twins. Biological scientists may only be looking at the physical DNA and predict if identical twins grew up separately in different environments they would still grow up with very similar attitudes, intelligence and abilities. That's not always the case. Studies show, for example, that if one of the twins grows up with homosexual tendencies you might expect the second twin to follow suit. However, statistics show often that is not the case. Scientists continue to accept their original paradigm though statistics prove differently. Social science and humanity do not always lend themselves to neat little packages as physical science does.

The sages of our past, while contemplating life and existence have come up with ideas that have revolutionized society making life more livable and understandable. That's inspiration also. Inspiration, to me is a profound insight hidden from the average un-attuned person. I believe a person emotionally and intellectually deeply engaged in living often picks up cues from his experiences and surroundings and is so "inspired" to suggest changes for the betterment of society. The Bible writers, for example, observing and writing about life pursuits and existence, expounded on principles of living not readily understood. They claimed it was 'God" speaking to them. How otherwise could they come up with wise insights, seemingly hidden to others and beyond their abilities? How else could they account for such clear and uncanny insights other than to say, "I must have been inspired by God?" And indeed, they were. So, "in tune" with the dream of something better, they accepted seemingly imperceptible guidance from the world, God's world, around them to come up with an uncanny understanding of life and human nature. The sages and prophets of Israel were moved to propose innovative ideas for dealing with poverty and equality as an example. To this day our advanced society can't figure out how to ensure equality; the rich keep getting richer and the poor poorer. That ancient society had a system so ingenious, so simple and yet so relevant to their agrarian society (called the Jubilee Year) that did insure long-term and fair equality. Outsiders might very well have admitted they were inspired. They claim to have perceived something coming from a higher source which they called "god." Those inspirations became the laws of the Israelites. Many dietary laws also could be deemed inspired and became part of the Jewish manual for living. Long before modern science discovered microorganisms, the leaders and sages of the Jewish people were inspired to write down laws for clean living, including dietary rules. Very interestingly, the Bible history informs us the average life span of a man was between seventy and eighty years (Psalm 90:10). It's only been relatively recently that average lifespans reached that level. It's taken hundreds of years of medical science to develop the technology to reach that level. The Bible writers weren't scientists, but they gleaned from careful observation aspects of healthy living. To me that's an example of divine (or higher power, if you wish) inspiration. Through observation and being attuned with God, with nature, or with that something beyond the perceivable, innovation occurred.

Here's one more line of reasoning that may appeal to some. I ask to what extent can a mind be trusted to accurately understand the concept of "mind?" What I'm questioning, for example, is to what extent can computer logic go beyond its capabilities to explain its own existence? The computer has limited mechanisms. That machine can only comprehend a limited number of concepts and, in fact, mainly mathematical based language. To what extent can mathematics explain human emotion or consciousness? Science admits a disconnect that cannot be explained as yet by current theory. That computer needs the assistance of a superior ability to go beyond itself, that ability being human ingenuity. Similarly, a human mind that reasons by chemical reactions only, according to science that's all there is, has limitations. To what extent will a person be willing to admit there might be concepts, like "god," they are not yet prepared to fully comprehend? Through the centuries there have always been thinkers willing to admit their mental limitations. Short of giving up, they posit a higher source for that ability. And that higher source may just be called "consciousness." I have noted that many scientists have begun to refer to God as simply "consciousness" or "awareness." Those are both operable terms to use in reference to God. Consciousness is the very simplest concept of God. Consciousness is a requisite of intelligence, of intention and purpose. As humans we have that consciousness and we ask, "When was it that this awareness came into existence? Did it have an origin or was it in existence from the infinite past?" For most thinkers, Consciousness always existing is the easiest alternative to accept rather than positing that "nothingness" existed before "somethingness." Either way, we each make a choice.

Getting back to my previously introduced idea of synergy, we can find there a source for abilities and insights beyond the individual mind. And this is something we can comprehend as one possible explanation of how God operates and what is included in God. Sociologists have long known that a baby born without assistance from an outside source is nothing more than a helpless animal. Without a society surrounding her she will always be devoid of higher capabilities like language, reasoning and communication. Learned culture from an intervening source is required for a baby to become more than an animal. The synergy of interaction allows her to become something beyond herself. Through the power of magnification and amplification by societies, individuals become greater than the sum of their parts. But to stop there, I would think, is short sighted. What about the synergy and interaction between humans and nature? Can there be an interaction between our planet as a living organism that can produce something beyond what we allow ourselves to believe possible? To where is that interaction leading? And what about the possibility of synergy in the Universe that could lead to a whole new inconceivable dimension? That's just the beginning, without debating whether there is a realm beyond the physical of which I firmly believe possible. Our present astounding discoveries provide the ability to comprehend the possible properties of something beyond human intelligence.

Furthermore, synergy works best when we avail ourselves of its power. When we labor in concert with and anticipate help from other sources, studies have shown more positive outcomes result. Denying this power leads to disappointing results. Similarly, all spiritual endeavors stress the importance of believing in its power. In the secular business world, many office settings anticipate and expect the power of synergy to work, though why it works is not fully understood. Spiritual practitioners in most religions are certain they feel a connection with something greater. To flatly deny the possibilities when we see clear evidence of positive outcomes on the social level appears to be shortsighted. Inspiration and synergy are two phenomena we observe continually. We cannot explain these phenomena by other means. Why cannot some accept the possibility they are a part of God or evidence of God?

It's so unfortunate that we live in a three-dimensional world. How much more could we comprehend if we weren't so bound? We've only begun to comprehend the possibilities of being able to work with and manipulate a fourth dimension, time. That ability would dramatically open up a whole new level of reality, being able to see the past as present and know the future ramifications of our present actions. Unfortunately, we're bound by the three dimensions. How foolish to claim our three-dimensional mind gives us all the tools necessary to make order out of reality.

Fortunately, sages and prophets and thinkers come along from time to time to offer profound insights, what we might call inspirations, to provide direction and an alternate and more realistic way of comprehending our world. Many scientists, like Newton, gave credit to something higher than themselves, inspiration from a source beyond. Our world has advanced due to the inspiration of Abraham Lincoln's Emancipation Proclamation, Martin Luther's inspired understanding of a more inclusive society and Martin Luther King's inspired "I have a dream" and recently Bill Gates' inspiration to help others realize that financial fortunes can be employed to eradicate world problems. These are all examples of inspiration beyond the common. These individuals had access to a higher source of

understanding no different from the prophets of old. Those prophets gave us principles of living to build on. Am I going to doubt
they were inspired by God or that those inspirations continue to
occur? Remember the STAR WARS films and their prophecies of
the future?   Lucas et al, not being particularly religious, speculated
that as far as we go technically and scientifically there still is room for
mysterious phenomena not readily understood. "May the FORCE
be with you!" That's basically what I mean when I say, "God be with
you!"   In fact, I think, if you watch the whole Star Wars series again,
you'll soon become a believer!

Chapter 4

The Age-Old Question
Why Suffering?

I invite you to spend time with me exploring what is perhaps the BIGGEST QUESTION in the study of religion: WHY SUFFERING? If there is a God, an all-powerful, benevolent God, why does he allow pain, suffering both physical and mental; accidents causing bodily injury with excruciating agony; babies born deformed and other disabilities; suffering from nature against man and man against man. That's probably the worst part, the cruelty of man toward man. We're going to present a clear, logical explanation with features you may have never considered before. This explanation follows a Christian line of thought but will be supplemented by findings from science and rational thought. And though it begins with a Christian perspective, the ideas are of universal appeal devoid of the terminology of any one religion or philosophy. My goal is to give you a plausible, logical explanation that is clear, satisfying and resolves most of the difficulties you may have found when contemplating this question. I can't give you all the answers, this life doesn't have ALL THE ANSWERS, even science does not have all the answers for any topic it studies and pure logic can only go so far. But I contend this presentation will finally, by follow a logical progression, provide clarity as to why, if there is a God, he allows such adversity.

FREE WILL

So here we go… Our question is this: Is the suffering in the world compatible with belief in a just, kind, and all- powerful God (the one nominally believed in by two thirds of the world's population)? The issue of whether there is a God at all is a separate study. But to even consider that question, for many, this question must be answered first, so we proceed. There is one idea that is at the center of this issue and is absolutely critical to our understanding here. This universe is built upon or exists with FREE WILL. Free will means rational beings have the ability to make choices. Actions are not totally influenced by instincts. For lower forms of life, a good deal of actions are based on automatic, conditioned responses. With humans we can choose to follow certain instincts or habits or we can choose to act differently. For example, all forms of life must take in nutrients to continue living. We as humans have the natural biological necessity to eat and we have automatic normal instincts and biological responses that remind us to eat (like a growling stomach), but we can choose not to eat. We can decide to go on a diet and not eat for periods of time. There is a difference between not eating due to one's feeling sick and rationally or emotionally choosing not to eat. The vast majority of the world's population believes in Free Will. The two main religions of the world (Christianity and Islam), which nominally makes up two thirds of the world population, posit the existence of Free Will.

Some philosophers and scientists, however, believe in what is called Determinism, where all activity is based on "Cause and Effect" and any reaction can be explained by a preceding reaction. That is always a possible premise, until you try to explain the FIRST CAUSE that started the Universe and the material world that could, to an extent, be explained by cause and effect. Where does Determinism fit in to the admitted fact that the Universe of material particles started with a "Big Bang?" The "material" for the Big Band had to proceed it per Determinism and that's a contradiction in itself. Furthermore, since the 1920's scientists have discovered from Quantum Physics what is termed The Heisenberg Uncertainty Principle. The discovery found that in the subatomic world, any action of the building blocks of atoms and molecules cannot be predicted with certainty. So even in miniscule particles chance (not Determinism) exists and the "momentum" and the position of a sub-atomic particle cannot be predicted accurately, they are based on probability or chance. If the actions of material building blocks of life cannot be predicted (CANNOT BE DETERMINED) with accuracy in the physical world, what does that indicate to us about the world they make up? We have also learned from the fields of Psychology and Sociology that there are too many variables to accurately predict the life course of any one individual. Furthermore, as a global civilization we inherently believe humankind has free will. For example, all societies believe in some sort of punishment for offenses that hurt other members of the community. This infers that we inherently believe in freewill. Punishment would be useless and meaningless if our actions were totally based on biology and the environment (Determinism). The vast majority of our world believes in free will whether they be religious or atheistic. Here, I've cited a number of arguments opposing the theory of Determinism and we could go in much more detail.

That is a whole discussion in itself that is laid out in any number of volumes found elsewhere so I must direct you to those studies since we cannot be side-tracked at the moment to expand on that topic.

Now, continuing with our reasoning, Christianity and the majority of World Religions teach that a Creator initially had a choice to either envision a race of robots or a race of rational, free will, autonomous beings. You'll note here I'm using a Christian example, but not trying to preach Christianity. I'm simply showing that a religious explanation can be based on logic too. When designing an organism "in god's-image," as Christianity teaches, God didn't really have much of a choice, though. Any human parents agree they would rather have children raised with free will as opposed to children unable to eventually live on their own, taking responsibility for their own lives. The main negative for God and such a decision is there is RISK involved. The more autonomy given to children, the more INHERENT RISK that they could hurt themselves or hurt each other. As a parent are you willing to take such a risk? That is the SAME decision a creator would make. The same decision we as parents conscientiously make and the same decision countless millions of parents make each year! Yes, human life could have been envisioned as a world of human robots. And yes, we can get a lot of fun out of a model train set but that has a limited appeal. The ultimate is a creature with free-will. A good part of the answer, to why if there is a god who allows evil, is answered by accepting free-will. If a human is allowed to make her own choices, a god must be prepared and would expect someone, some time would make the wrong choice, wrong being a choice that hurts her or those around her. So, whose fault is that? Is it really God's fault? Fault is not the correct word, here; this is a consequence not a fault. This is not a blame issue; it is a cause and effect reality! As I remind you, I'm arguing from a rational view and a Christian view but the basic tenets are found in most all societies that prescribe deterrents and punishments. The fact that most all philosophies also agree with the necessity of punishment indicates the tacit acceptance of free will as being a given. There are several religions that may not, perhaps due to their founders feeling the concept of an all-powerful but loving God allowing suffering would be too difficult to explain. They proceeded in the contrary direction, assuming all life is predetermined (Determinism). The difficulty with this reasoning is having to answer a whole new set of questions as we alluded to in the previous paragraphs. We can't have it both ways, either we have robots or we have humans permitted to make choices that may constitute evil! One of the beauties of Christianity is Jesus' concept of picturing God as our Father. This personification of God makes Him more real and is a concept the human mind can readily comprehend and work with. Two thirds of our modern world (Christianity and Islam) see such an all-powerful caring God. Even Plato, before Christ and Mohammed, reasoned that somewhere there must be a spiritual world; there had to be a "Father" that was the epitome of a perfect human father we seek to replicate.

Unfortunately, though at least 75% of the world believe in a God of some sort, his picture is skewed by diverse human experience and culture. Is God predominately angry, aloof, foreboding, selfish, and demanding of complete control and obedience? What Jesus taught was God as the perfect, caring, loving, wise Father, the one we had, or wished we had, while we were growing up. If, then, we believe in the possibility of such a wise father, then we assume there must be a perfectly good reason why He allows adversity. And again, the one quality required to make sense of this scenario is the concept of Free Will. Humans who have this ability to think, decide, evaluate and act have that Free Will. Jesus' pictures of God permit us to relate to something which might be beyond our mental comprehension otherwise. Note his picture is not of a perfectionist Father, a domineering father, but a father who wants his children to have the excitement of experiencing life and learning from that experience. At the same time this Father protects his children from undue suffering with personal guidance and advice. Similarly, our biological father knows we will make mistakes, accepts this, but expects the best for his children in the end. That was Jesus' message too. I don't think most humans would want it any other way!

THE SURVIVAL PRINCIPLE

The next concept required to make sense of pain and sorrow is one that everyone has experienced in life and one that science has verified through countless experiments and observations. I caution that some Christians may resist accepting this observation, at first, but will realize it's not a threat to their faith but just another take on a concept they are very familiar with. This is a life principle found in every living organism. All living things have built within them (if you believe in God, you might say "built into them") the resources necessary to do whatever necessary to SURVIVE AT ALL COSTS. Without this principle at work, no living thing could survive for long! Think of it this way. Every living thing must have mechanisms for the species to survive beyond one generation. The simplest amoeba, a virus, a one celled organism, a mouse, any animal, any plant has the mechanisms it needs to survive. That's why we see a world teaming with millions of diverse organisms with diverse structures and instincts. Every living thing is simultaneously fighting for its survival. This concept is especially notable in humans too. This concept in itself explains part of the CONFLICT and adversity in our world, doesn't it? Can you see that there must be conflict to some degree, there is no other way?

If every living organism is "programmed" or bent on surviving and is fighting for its share of life resources, there is bound to be conflict. The only other possibility is a world that is built in the fashion of a grand machine, a toy for its creator who winds it up and WATCHES IT PLAY out its expected routine over and over again. I can't see any kind of creator or The Creator ever being content with that kind of world. We all know little children get bored with their presents and toys usually within one day! Why do our kids play with the boxes the toys come in longer than the toys themselves? We enjoy unpredictability, invention, innovation, ingenuity. A believer in a higher power would say life was envisioned that way. While an unbeliever would say it's just fortunate life evolved that way with the Universe just happening to start out with a goal seeking survival mechanism built in by pure chance from somewhere or nowhere (that's a discussion for another time, though).

Either way, the result is all material living existence has an inherent conflict/survival mechanism built within. Each organism is determined to live, survive, flourish. Survival is inherent in the universe. The trait of inherent self-interest may be interpreted by some as selfishness but in reality, this is a preservation mechanism that humans, like all living things must possess. Really it's all a matter of semantics; for example, to believe that we are "special" as the Bible claims we are, some might interpret the word "special" as claiming humanity is inherently selfish whereas psychology has come to find and would prefer to use the term "a good self-esteem (realistic self-concept)," as opposed to the word "selfishness" as a necessary ingredient of a well-functioning person. That may be hard to accept, but it is the only logical conclusion. If we believe in an all-knowing God, we must accept he knew in advance suffering would eventually be part of our world. In a moment we will discuss why such a God would decide this would be the best possible situation, all things considered. What Christianity teaches is that though conflict, suffering, pain can be expected, some of the effects can be prevented and mitigated. We'll talk more about that later also.

All major religions have their own traditions and explanations as to why there is pain and agony in our world. Some have NOT been able to equate an all-powerful, caring God with the pain. These religions speak of God only in the sense of a force, an all-pervading power or simply Karma. However, as we mentioned, most of the world believes in a caring God. To illustrate, I'll turn to one explanation, the Christian Tradition, as a suggested possibility as to how and why such a God could allow affliction and agonizing death. You'll find when you examine the scriptural references, they are clear and reasonable with few loose ends left to be tied up. There can never be perfect clarity, however, because any human explanation can only be put in human, material terms bound by time and space. A more accurate accounting would require understanding timelessness and a spatial approach unbounded by the physical and material. Unfortunately, we are not thus equipped. So as Plato, mentioned earlier, used the illustration of humans like cave dwellers only able to see the shadows of reality, so true of our circumstance. In fact, current Post- Modern Philosophy has much less of a problem with this religious idea since they have discovered that most of our problems with dialog between various interest groups is due to language. Based on each person's individual life-experience, the same word has different connotations based on each person's life experience. And when we add space and time into the discussion, all of us have very limited experience with the full ramifications of such a reality. Please follow this explanation from Christian scripture, you'll find, even if you are a Christian, the explanation may be somewhat different than you personally may have formulated it in the past.

Here is the Biblical explanation of Why suffering. What I'm attempting to show is that the explanation is logical. Logic is not a proof but a plausible explanation that makes sense, and that is what this treatise is all about, finding a plausible explanation for evil and suffering. The very first book of the Bible, in the first chapter, gives us the background we need. Here we find the story of Adam and Eve and herein we have provided three factors that explain the human predicament. First these humans were created (or evolved if your faith is in all-encompassing material particles, excuse my bias) with FREE WILL. The first couple had choices to make, choices that affected the rest of their lives. Next, from the beginning the Bible notes that humans without prior experience or an environment of evil were capable of evil. Note, these humans deemed "perfect" specimens, from human standards, were capable of evil because of the GIFT of CHOICE. Per scripture, the source of all evil or suffering is due to human choice and another creature, a serpent, who had already made a contrarian choice, in this particular account. And as hinted previously, all livings things, including this pair, have that inherent tendency for survival and personal self-interest and welfare (the serpent appealed to self-interest already built into humanity.) These findings are crucial in our understanding since the majority of suffering is brought on by humans against humans. In error, people often take actions based on what they think will benefit themselves in the short run only to find in the long run they have actually hurt themselves and others. So often parents take an expedient action, not realizing they will irreparably hinder family, community, states and then countries, perpetuating suffering for generations. How many countless millions have been maimed and killed due to war and ensuing property damage and cruel treatment by the powers that be? Resorting to manipulation and control. This is not God's doing. True, He had to envision mechanisms such as sexual appeal to ensure procreation and self-interest to ensure a desire to survive. The stronger that desire to survive the more likely the organism will flourish.

However, the Bible is unequivocal in asserting that God does not cause evil nor tempts one with evil. As stated, "When tempted let no one say, 'God is tempting me.'" For God cannot be tempted, nor does he tempt anyone; but each one is tempted when, by his own desires, he is dragged away and enticed." (James 1:12-4) Throughout the Bible there are instances when individuals assumed God was tempting or causing evil to fall on them, but James makes it clear this is not God's doing but the consequence of "his own desires," self-interest desires. And as we asserted, no organism could survive for long without the self-interest mechanism built in.

Another point is clear from the Bible account. Early on, mankind realized one of their major tasks in living in the material world was to "fill the earth and subdue it." (Genesis 1:28). Humans now are beginning to realize that we're required to "subdue nature." All nature, as we know today, has a mind of its own so to speak. Nature has that survival mechanism built within. As we already deduced, life could not exist without this apparently "selfishly-survival" component. The original Bible account records that ages ago the ancients realized suffering could be caused by nature and one of their human goals would always be to "subdue the earth," "subdue nature." We're only beginning to understand that "subdue nature" requires living in harmony with nature. For instance, how much agony could be avoided if builders didn't insist on building dwellings in known flood zones? Or how much distress could be circumvented by not building on the side of known volcanos? How much suffering could be avoided by making provisions for hurricane winds and the hazards of lightning fires? Subduing nature gives the connotation of adversity being involved, doesn't it? A listener back then would take this directive to mean mankind was intended to be busy working. Subduing anything is not always an easy task. The implication being that humans would have hard work, but with a meaningful, beautiful goal. Until the Earth and nature were subdued this portended difficulty ahead. Our ancestors evidently didn't think there was a conflict between a loving God expecting his progeny to encounter difficulties in life, even in this, one of the first stories our ancestors learned and related to their children. To this day most parents expect their children to go through difficulties as part of growing up. Something here is hinting God's intent was for those living to expect to have hardships and difficulties and that this would give life meaning.

I know that seems simplistic, but the Bible is unequivocal in asserting the Christian perspective tells us the majority of suffering is caused by human desires and the negligence of protecting and subduing nature. Fortunately, we are beginning to learn to protect against disease (e.g. heart disease) and sickness. Whose fault is it that the obesity rate in the US is approaching fifty percent? Who's responsible for the suffering caused by diabetes, heart disease, emphysema and other sources of natural suffering? That's not counting the pain caused by the human ability to give free reign and not sequester our "desires." Furthermore, scripture tells us God expected this from the beginning of time. Sorrow, affliction, pain was anticipated as a consequence of free will and the teeming life force and diverse survival mechanisms necessary in nature. I quote here the Bible writer who understood clearly that "before the beginning of time" God foresaw the challenges humans would face and the plan needed to face it. "This grace was given us in Christ Jesus before the beginning of time." (1Timothy 1:10) However, provisions were put in place initially by God to make it easier to bear up under suffering and also guidance to avoid affliction

LESSONS TO BE LEARNED FROM SUFFERING

And here's the AMAZING PART! There is a lesson to be learned from the ever-present threat of suffering. There is a lesson that every spiritual person at some point begins to grasp. In fact, this is one of the many conundrums spiritual wisdom teaches. THERE IS ALWAYS A GOOD SIDE TO WHATEVER BAD OCCURS! Christians are taught, though many don't learn the lesson until later in life (sometimes never in this life), the lesson-LOOK FOR THE GOOD SIDE. Look for how sorrow, once you've lived through it, makes you a better person and assists you in controlling your selfish tendencies and begin to perceive more clearly the spiritual side of life. In rapid succession I'll run through some of the testimonies of people who have gone through suffering and realized how it transformed their lives for the better. There are countless examples, testimonies from both famous and ordinary people like you and me. What happened to Ignatius of Loyola has happened millions of times. He tells us that when he was convalescing from an injury from the battlefield, through his pain and agony, he was forced to contemplate life. He too asked, "Why Suffering?" and what he could do to help those in desolation and poverty. He was moved to help the poor and in fact started a movement within the Catholic Church to help the poor called the Society of Jesus. To this day the "Jesuits" are noted for their concern for the poor and for the need of education for all. The church commemorated the founder by referring to him as St. Ignatius. The point is Ignatius would never have contemplated his life without suffering.

A beautiful fraternity devoted to the poor and uneducated would not have come to be without suffering.

Read for yourself the lesson Tim Tebow, the once well-known football player learned. I happened to read his book a little while back. The difficulties he went through were not so momentous as Ignatius' but yet were ones most of us have lived through and can relate to. He lost his job, actually three or four jobs. Unfortunately, because he was well known, his predicament was plastered all over the sports news. How humiliating! He confided, "It was tough to live through some painful moments, But I'll say in those places of doubt and even of darkness, I've realized that who I am has nothing to do with wins and losses, applause or negative criticism. It has to do with who I am." (SHAKEN, Waterbrook Publisher, NY, 2017) Similarly, a good friend confided in me when, first diagnosed with leukemia (an earth-shattering experience). "I realize this is one of the best things that ever happened to me. I have been living with no meaning in my life. I have let my life, while I was in good health, pass me by. I only now realize how thankful for my health I should have been. How much time I squandered taking my ideal circumstances for granted." This realization and prayer for guidance put him on the road to recovery though only time will tell his survival capacity. And, though redundant, I too can testify to what I personally learned. For my whole life before I had major trauma, I was convinced I could always find a way to overcome my problems if I tried hard enough. Finally, when faced with a dying heart (cardiomyopathy) I understood full well I needed help from outside myself, I admitted I could only do so much by myself. More than ever I have asked for and received assistance from a higher power. We all know friends and associates who can testify with their own moving stories. And since there are hundreds of books written on the subject of Adversity and its benefits, written from both a spiritual and secular testament, I direct you to any of these. There you will find thousands of accounts of how the willingness to confront difficulties can transform adversity from a handicap to an asset. It would be unnecessary to spend more time recounting them here.

However, in deference to my fellow Christian friends, many of whom have not been taught to look at the positive side to adversity, I refer to three different Bible writers who discovered the same lesson from their personal experiences and from their Master, Jesus. These writers were attempting to understand the reason for evil and suffering from their own experiences. James, in his book, put it like this, "Consider it PURE JOY my brothers when you face trials of many kinds…" and adds "[by] the testing quality [those trials] makes you complete." (James 1:2-4) James talks to us of trials of MANY KINDS whether sickness, persecution, homelessness, hunger, poverty, on and on. Note that James confirms life is filled with "trials of different kinds." He and the apostles of Jesus faced all types of trials. St. Paul speaks of shipwrecks, poverty, beatings, loss of friends and loved ones. What they learned is that these trials made them better people. James speaks here of the "Testing of your faith." He is hinting at the idea behind the "why" of testing from suffering and the reasons behind testing. Think for a moment, the Bible frequently assures us that God already knows a person's heart or disposition. He doesn't need to do any testing to assay an individual's true being and level of faith. He can predict a person's disposition perfectly. Even we, as humans, without seeing a person's inner workings can very often predict a person's actions by what that person says or how he acts in inconsequential settings. Given that, how certain we can be God knows each of us in much finer detail and actually can commune with our thoughts. The point is this, God doesn't need to do any testing, he already knows. Testing is primarily for OUR BENEFIT. Difficult situations we confront expose to ourselves who we are! Going through trials we expose ourselves to ourselves primarily but to others on a secondary basis. We learn from such experiences only if we choose to learn. We see ourselves for whom we really are, if we are willing to take note and admit to ourselves the good and the not so good within. How often have you learned about yourself from your perseverance, as James used the example? You've persevered through a sickness and didn't give in. You stuck with a friend through her trials. You persevered to get an education. It wasn't easy but you did it. These experiences build character and help you to see who you are and what you are capable of. You may not be as miserable a human specimen as you think after all. In fact, you might actually feel good about yourself upon reflection.

Conversely, you may not pass some of those little tests along the way. Like when you blow your cool, totally losing it with a friend or even a sales clerk. This is an occasion to learn. You realize there's an aspect of your life you might need to improve. Can you see there is no other way or, at least, very limited opportunity to "test" yourself, or learn about yourself without pain and suffering? I have to ask, is there really any other way? Living in a perfect world with no trials would never allow you to truly know your capabilities, your various qualities. The goal of all this effort, says James, is "so that you may be mature and complete, not lacking anything." (James 1:4) There you have it, in James' estimation and based on his experience with Jesus, suffering is necessary to help nurture us to a level of "maturity," to be "complete" as humans. ADVERSITY IS NECESSARY TO BUILD CHARACTER AND VIRTUE. Having only pleasurable experiences day by day is not enough for complete training in becoming a child of God the Father. Isn't it true we admire any elder member of our community who has gone through diverse, difficult life experiences both good and bad? He has learned from experience how to confront all the inconsistencies of life? All-encompassing wisdom would require learning from adversity, being refined as if going through a smelter's fire to purify the precious metals within, as Scripture uses the illustration. Ask now, "Could I be complete in all ways without the experience of having faced adversity?" I don't think it's possible! But isn't it wonderful and kind that the master of our Faith, Jesus, always reminds us of the "Up Side," "You will weep and mourn... you will grieve but your grief will turn to joy?" (John 16:20)

In my estimation, it is so unfortunate that more people have never been prepared for anguish and affliction by having had it explained to them what they are trying to accomplish by undergoing such ordeals. Can we also deduce that if we keep in mind why God allows suffering, during the time while suffering, it's a little easier to cope with the pain knowing why it's necessary? I know from experience I can handle the pain involved while healing from an ailment much more easily if I know the end result will improve my health. Knowing what God has in mind for us (expanding our capabilities and our outlook of standing before the Lord as a complete, finished product, refined in every way) assists us in maintaining the fortitude to bear up under distress. Who knows, you may actually be willing to volunteer for such a painful assignment? If only more people could open their eyes and see what is really being accomplished when they live through difficulties. They would begin to look at travail more as an inconvenience in the short run. If you are a parent, you have the task of helping your children understand life requires they go through years of schooling to emerge as a competent member of society able to comprehend and deal with all manner of life eventualities. You and your children would probably have rather foregone the years of going to school daily if you had a choice. "There's got to be any easier way," you used to say. No, there wasn't and no, there isn't. I think it is so unfortunate that children are not taught in school, and parents often don't teach their children, the simple profound message that misery and sorrow are building blocks for success in life. Tell them the truth! "My son, you will learn who you are and appreciate your uniqueness by going through sorrow. I wish I could do it for you but I can't. You'll never be a mature and a fully functioning man without some agony in your life."

Now listen to another writer's life experience and his insight. Paul, an apostle of Jesus, lived through his share of adversity. He recounts with satisfaction his ordeal at 2 Corinthians 1:8-10 "The hardships we suffered in the province of Asia. We were under great pressure, far beyond our ability to endure, so we despaired even of life. Indeed, in our hearts we felt the sentence of death." There is an important lesson emphasized in his story. He attempted to make sense of it all, asking just as you and I are now asking, "Why?" Using the wisdom garnered from his trials he could say confidently, "But this happened (His own words) that we might not rely on ourselves but on God, who raises the dead." Here, Paul proposes yet another reason why we must despair at times. The additional lesson is to learn to rely on God. Can you see there could never be a more indelible method of having this lessen impressed on us than by experiencing situations where we have no other place to turn? I've had this happen many times but perhaps the most enlightening was the time I found myself flat on my back on a hospital bed, unable to even move, unable to do anything for myself, taking a breath was an effort. Confessing to myself I said, "I finally get it, I can't do anything, anything on my own any longer, I admit I need help!" Within a few hours my confession was, "I know now, I can't live any longer, pretending I can do everything all on my own." To this day whenever I meet adversity, I automatically respond by saying, "I can't do this alone, I need your help!" I'm learning the lesson Paul learned centuries ago. And perhaps there is no other way to learn it. There are times we must rely on God. We can't do it on our own. Adversity is not really an enemy after all, is it?

Here is still another observation from Paul when he states (Romans 5:3-5), "But we REJOICE IN OUR SUFFERINGS because we know that suffering produces perseverance, perseverance, character; and character, hope. And hope does not disappoint us." Here the apostle tells us there is no other way through this progression but with adversity. To master perseverance, one must confront troubles. Those troubles make us stronger and give us determination. A point comes, as we stick with it, where pain is not a detriment. Getting through to the end becomes our concern. Most all of us have, I hope, felt the exhilaration of reaching a worthy goal. Nothing quite compares to that feeling. There is no other way to get that particular joy without expending ourselves for a worthy goal. Anyone reaching the goal, whether its school graduation or finishing a difficult project, most always will say that the adversity was worth all the trouble. The apostle presumes anyone having the hope that he can conquer suffering "will not be disappointed." No one confronting pain looks forward to it, many don't even think they could endure, but somehow, they do. I can say, most everyone who has ever confided in me and discussed his/her ordeals with me, testified that that his/her comprehension of the meaning of life profoundly expanded and what was discovered about his/her self completely agreed with the apostle's assessment, it's worth it!

Before moving on, we must dwell for a moment on the prize endurance offers. Paul says, "Perseverance begets character." CHARACTER, we don't hear much about that term these days. In days gone by character was especially prized. Our western civilization was built upon that foundation. The Bible lauds it and even the Greek heritage that gave us the impetus to search for knowledge and the concept of democracy highlighted character. To Aristotle, the Greek, virtue and character were the most prized of personal characteristics of a person. To be a person of character was the epitome of human growth then, but unfortunately pleasure has displaced character as the major goal in our society. And, very interestingly, our level of happiness has diminished generation by generation over time in modern times, studies have concluded. True self-esteem requires character. Character is the state of making a good habit so automatic it becomes second nature. Character produces dignity, confidence and strength. That's the type of person our Father foresaw for humankind and it is the epitome of humanity he wants for each of us to attain. Evidently there is no better way to attain that highest standard without inconvenience and trials.

A person, having gone through this purging, is a better person, a fuller person, because of faith one has built. If you've gone through this metamorphosis, you don't believe in a life hereafter just because someone told you to believe. For all you knew, when you started the journey of Christianity, that was "pie in the sky." But you took the step, you endured, you persevered through trials, you proved that with God's help you could confront and conquer a lot more than you originally thought possible. Now your faith is "genuine." No one can accuse you of being gullible, you proved to yourself that your faith is based on experience. That faith is going to carry you through for as long as there is a you. Faith to confront future adversity, faith that you will reach seemingly unattainable heights. You now have the faith that you're ready for any privileged assignments coming your way in the future. All because you did the unthinkable... you suffered.

GUIDANCE THROUGH THE SUFFERING

Here's the final ingredient in the suffering formula. There is a way, all religions contend, believers can mitigate agony by accepting assistance during times of sorrow. Christianity calls this help God's Spirit and even science fiction writers approximate it by speaking of "The Force." There is a source of power, energy and strength available to overcome travail and pain. Somehow, someway, believers can come through without the lasting effects of trauma. Jesus called the Spirit "The Helper." The God Christians believe in may allow agony but offers comfort, superhuman endurance and determination along the way. Most everyone who agonizes over injustice is encouraged to pray the prayer of Ephesians 4:7 and will sense "The Peace of God, which transcending all understanding, will guard your hearts and minds in Christ Jesus" during the hours of personal trials. The anecdotal studies I've done and the full research studies others have done, confirm this promise. Non-believers who have not had the privilege of experiencing this sensation may doubt but are not in any position to contradict someone's own testimony who has actually lived the experience. The non-believer cannot speak on a matter he has no personal experience of than to doubt the possibilities.

Quickly, though, let me present what is the BEST PART of what is to be discovered. Through sorrows, seekers of comfort and direction are not left in the lurch. A spiritual outlook offers all the tools needed to overcome difficulties. I'll mention but three or four ways here, but there are many more. For example, the Christian way gives a set of simple principles for living to pattern one's life by. It is amazing that most every situation that could arise is covered in the three short chapters in the Bible called the Sermon on the Mount (Matthew chapter 5 through 7). So simple, so concise, almost everything you need to know about living through the happy times and the unsettling times. In fact, many of these principles are presented in other religions and other societies independently. This is a testimony to the universality of Jesus' guidance. Given are thoughts on the worthiest goals of life and how to handle difficult situations that arise. By living accordingly, a good portion of the evils in the world are mitigated by the advice here. Potential evils, their effects and long-term eventualities of adversity, can be minimized. At least, I and millions of others can so testify. Yes, we suffer but not unbearably. A spiritual person acknowledges pain, suffering, and agony as unavoidable but serving a purpose. And there are ways to cope. The Bible itself contains hundreds of examples of real people throughout history who have conquered, overcome the most agonizing of possible events and yet kept their positive perspective through all. These real people can offer guidance to negotiate the mine fields of obstacles strewn throughout life's journey.

Finally, I've discovered that just understanding the "Why" of Suffering and the GOOD one can expect from such ordeals aids in making it so much easier to face and endure the pain. I'm sure all of us have experienced when warned of a coming problem and instructed on what to expect and how to handle the discomfort, we find it so much easier to face. This calls to mind my personal experiences of going to foreign countries. I've been warned that most of the citizens in a particular country don't speak English. But a friend might suggest, "This is where you can always go to find someone who does speak English. And these are the few word phrases you must know before you go." I've gone through this experience several times, some with and some without the forewarnings and suggestions. Always experiences when armed with foresight were much easier to handle. This is precisely why Jesus warned (John 16:20), "You will grieve but your grief will turn to joy." Coupled with his instructions on how to live through pain, the travail is endurable. For example, scripture tells us the worst thing we can do when suffering is to feel sorry for ourselves. When not taken by surprise and when prepared, the plight is more endurable. In the above verse Jesus prefaced his comments on grief by saying, "You will weep and mourn while the world rejoices." You will feel all alone, it will appear everyone else in the world is having a good time. And be assured mental pain can have worse consequences than any physical pain. Being right with God and right with self is sweet even in the midst of pain. Sages claim, through their examples, you can endure most anything with a personal sense of integrity and with divine strength.

SUMMARY

Now, here's what we accomplished so far. We've seen, from a logical standpoint suffering is NOT INCOMPATIBLE with there being an Almighty God who cares. We've seen that it's REASONABLE, though not completely provable, that a "Father God" would allow adversity as any parent would for his/her children. We've seen that suffering is INVALUABLE. We personally gain capabilities, insights, PERSONAL GROWTH in addition to FAITH, CHARACTER and personal insights we could gain in NO OTHER WAY! Do we have all the answers? No, we stated at the onset it would be impossible to have all the answers. We're not privy to the mental and metaphysical ability and haven't experienced the necessary longevity to see the full picture or the final exposition of human civilization's run. We have only an incomplete picture, but this needn't discourage us. Historical narratives and experience from the field of science often start by revealing partial answers without total understanding, but in time there is more clarity. Certainly, there is at least enough background evidence for the "why of trials" to eliminate millions from ever doubting there could be a God and the resultant sense of alone-ness. And that's all God is asking of us, Don't Give Up! How many times have you said to your children or your parents have said to you, "Wait till you grow up, it will all make sense then? Just trust me now; as you experience life it becomes clearer!"

My premise in assembling these ideas is to demonstrate we have enough of an answer to this age-old question of why pain and suffer-ing to perceive a little clarity. My explanation has taken into account the biological reality, mental reality and the spiritual reality of our existence. Not a full picture, but enough of a picture to base a life on. Enough of an understanding to make informed decisions. And as we will see, enough of a picture to have an optimistic outlook to live without resentment. I personally am a rather demanding person. I pride myself in not being gullible. I've never accepted ideas without first checking their accuracy and the logical reasoning behind them. Over the years I have had to reorganize and edit my views so they better coincide with the real world. The picture presented here sat-isfies my need for rigor, I hope yours too. You'll note I have left out the usual religious terms used in a discussion on suffering, terms like "sin and salvation." Not because they are unimportant but because I wanted to focus on one issue and one issue only for now. These other terms are relevant but part of another discussion. I hope your under-standing of suffering is clearer as a result.

To those of you not Christian, this may only be an interesting explanation, nothing more at this point. But this might help. I was exposed to the comment I'm about to make by arguably the most respected and renowned secular philosopher of all times, Immanuel Kant. He was the thinker that helped put science back on solid foot-ing when philosophers first admitted that it was impossible to prove anything absolutely, beyond any doubt. So why put faith in science or anything else for that matter? Kant gave a very detailed stance and what appealed to me is this. In affect Kant argued (presented in my words) "Sure, we have absolutely no unassailable proof of anything in this world; faith is required for whatever you believe but if a position is REASONABLE and makes sense logically there is an element of truth there and that position is worthy of following through to see if it leads to uncorrectable contradictions or is to be deemed sound argumentation." This has always been my own position on questions of life and existence. And, in fact, that's why I'm a Christian after all these many years of life experience. Christianity makes sense and social research has exonerated its stance over the years in all areas of science, psychology, sociology and physical science as they make their discoveries. Christianity has stood the test of time. My submission here on suffering does not include all answers any more than any area of science or philosophy can claim to have all the answers. But the Christian position is logical and leads to practical, useable conclusions.

PRACTICAL APPLICATION

Now, how can this knowledge be used constructively? And this, too, is a benefit of Christianity, providing a way of life that helps one live in a suffering world. It is true, other religions provide their own explanations and all of them have common elements with the Christian position. Though I have admitted repeatedly I don't have all the answers, but for me, the Christian viewpoint is the most complete, optimistic and energizing. The end is not a Nirvana or state of Equipoise where all existence ends in an equilibrium. Confronting such an end may not be as satisfying as the Christian Finale that includes a living world of true justice, peace, endless opportunities for discovery and adventure. Sorry, I can only give a Christian outlook here since I have studied it thoroughly to detect any inconsistencies and have actually lived it for a lifetime to prove its practicality. I can say it really works. Of course, I've had to adjust my views over the years; life experience forces us to correct some of our original simplistic ideals along the way. For me the Christian worldview has become more complete, satisfying and durable over the years.

As mentioned, and you'll notice I don't appeal to some of the usual Christian terms here, like sin, punishment, salvation or perfection. Over the years, men have misused these terms to control and scare at times. They are very important terms and presented in the Bible as facts of life and explanations of reality. But I feel in order to focus on one momentous idea, suffering, we've had to put off discussing other areas of practical living. And when talking of pain, be assured, mental pain is as difficult as physical pain.

GETTING BACK TO THE HARD PART

I know, you may be thinking "All well and good. But what about the little babies and the poor innocents forced to face inhuman conditions?" At the very beginning we asserted why suffering is necessary. Free will is one of the culprits. Nature's inherent physical survival mechanisms mandate suffering as one life form gets in the way of another's need to survive. But couldn't God do more to help? Couldn't God give everyone a choice; Do you want to be born as an animal with instincts and robotic responses or would you rather have free will and a mind to analyze events, to contemplate beauty, to invent and write your own story? That's not very realistic. First of all, wouldn't you have to have experienced free will first even to make an informed choice? I'd wager, if we asked the question of people anyway, maybe you'd find one in a million preferring to say they'd rather be that animal. Of those suffering now, ask the question when they have a moment of reprieve from their pain and again, you'd find few wanting to live in the wilds happy to roam with plentiful food around you. The God the majority of the world are familiar with, in his wisdom and foresight, who is claimed to know everyone, makes the claim that under better conditions most all humans would be ecstatic with free will, unlimited choices, and endless options though having to endure pain and suffering at times.

But babies don't get a choice, do they? Here's a partial response. When they cry it's almost as if they are crying out for justice. That's a reason why, Immanuel Kant, the secular philosopher, confessed there must be an all-powerful, caring God who only could rectify this type of agony. Justice demands, he reasoned, since for many babies their parents or progenitors are the culprits causing the child's suffering by making personal choices (there's that FREE-WILL, again) that presumably makes life easier for themselves but hurts the helpless. Universally, humans understand what justice entails. Kant reasoned from a purely logical angle, since we all inherently want justice there has to be an afterlife where all injustices will be rectified. And let me interject a small point here. The Bible claims God wants all to live happily in a realm of harmony and beauty. Living through our present world, we could never take for granted such a just world since we have lived through a contrasting world of evil. If that were true, ask the formerly suffering person now at some future point once restored without overwhelming pain, "Was the suffering worth it?" I'd want to know their answer to this other part of the question, "Are you a better person today for what you endured?" I think you know the answers they'd probably give. However, I must admit, this incidence of babies suffering at birth is still unsettling. And this is all I can say at this point. To me, this aspect is one of the "few loose-ends" toward a satisfying answer to our question. But, by the same token, I admit to myself, I feel I have a satisfying answer to the major part of our initial question, so I can't discount what I know to be logical for the one dangling aspect I can't fully understand. Furthermore, let me say, Christianity does have a logical answer for this issue, but one requiring more religious conceptions that I admitted I would not bring into this discussion. Something I will be happy to present at another time.

We are inferring that as humans, we are fully able to answer the question of suffering. And a person with even a modicum of faith might ask our question differently. Yes, faith is the wild card here. Free of the restraints of our disadvantaged vantage point in this struggling world, faith gives us more avenues to explore. I can mention my own life journey here. I started out when young a nobody, knowing nothing. Being shy and not knowing where to turn, I read a passage in the Bible (Matthew 6:33 to be exact) promising if I sought first God's Kingdom, everything I would ever need would be given me. Having nothing to lose, I accepted the challenge. That acceptance has provided me with everything I ever have needed in my life and many of the wants too for good measure. Pain, yes, excruciating pain, suffering too in the extreme, but all worth it as I come to the point where I am beginning to see the top of the mountain I've been climbing all these years.

I hope this discussion is a good starting point for you to contemplate this vital issue. You need to be the final judge as to whether there is enough evidence to allow you to identify what the implications are for you in your search for a meaningful, satisfying life. If you haven't yet made a decision on whether you believe in a god, at least you have logical reasons to proceed in your search. If you already believe in a god, now you have every reason to proceed more deeply into what this God is really like and if he really does assist you in living as claimed. For most individuals who have gone down a spiritual path, this question of why God allows suffering have found, over time, it no longer to be an issue. A Spiritual Life allows those experiencing the effects of trauma to trust in God's mercy and kindness. They have come to know that God is a good and merciful friend as Jesus assures rhetorically, "How much more will your Father in heaven give good gifts to those who ask him?" (Matthew 7:11) We spent this time talking of the negatives of life but what do you think? Really, aren't there far more good things in life than the negatives? I think so.

Once we realize Adversity in this Life is a rational expectation, that adversity is an absolute necessity and it has so many benefits, we can calmly accept the reality and live in reality. Jesus had this in mind when he counsels us, "In the world you will have trouble, but take heart, I have conquered the world." (John 16:33) Don't be obsessed with your troubles but be confident you too will overcome them as millions of others have already affirmed.

Chapter 5

Doctor Faust And The King

You probably have heard the story of Doctor Faust. He's the gentlemen who purportedly sold his soul to the devil. Here's the real story. The Doctor was actually a good guy, he just wanted answers. There are several versions of the story so we'll stick with the most famous written by Johann Wolfgang von Goethe. Goethe is the German poet and writer who is to the German language what Shakespeare is to English. He's the epitome of German authors. Immediately upon reading the story, one can't help but think of the Bible story of Job. However, what readers never realize, this story actually is the story of King Solomon of Bible fame.

Here's the background. First, you probably know the story of Job in the Bible. Remember Job loses everything, his wealth, his family, even his health. Then his would-be friends, though trying to console him at first, insinuate Job must have done something really wicked to find himself in such an extreme position. They had the impression, the same impression some have today, that if you are faithful to God your life would be blessed and you could expect only blue skies ahead. However, most individuals today realize that is spurious reasoning. The "blessed" part is true but the "blue skies" part can't be counted on. The Good do experience evil and disappointments, no different from Agnostics and those who are disinterested in God.

What's more, in Job's case, we are informed that behind the scenes Job was subjected to a test of a sort without his knowledge. Not just Job, but all humanity, the story implies, are being scrutinized. Job's story took place back in the days when Satan, who is called Mephistopheles in Goethe's version, was on speaking terms with God. In the book of Job, Satan confronts God with a challenge. He asserts Job, a well-known believer in God, was only faithful due to all the blessings God bestowed upon him. "Take it all away and he'll curse you to your face, God," he boasted. That claim really applies to all humans, not just to Job. All humans are defective is the contention and would never remain faithful to God if tested. In Goethe's story, God is the one starting the conversation about Faust. "Yes, humans all make mistakes, including Doctor Faust, but there will always be some humans who will be able to distinguish between Good and Evil and choose the good," God emphatically alleges.

In Job's case, he, as the protagonist, did not realize what was happening. In Goethe's version, Mephistopheles come to Faust and plays the part of a confidant, claiming to help the Doctor. Now, as you also know, in the Bible account Job passed the test. He did not curse God as it was claimed he would but remained faithful. Only then was it revealed to him that he, Job, had been the subject of a dispute between God and the Evil One.

There are several salient points to draw from the story. First, all humans, having the same heritage from the same Source (God), have the same inherited capacity of knowing Good from Bad. Therefore, there will always be some, like Job, who will seek the Good and cherish the moral character we were all born to exhibit. Second, the story helps us to understand the Bigger Question, the one everyone asks, "Why, if there is a God, does he allow wickedness?" The Bible answer, from the book of Job, is that there are events happening behind the scenes that humans are not privy to. There is also an Evil presence in the world due to the fact humans have free-will and can choose their actions, Good or Evil. Events happen all around us, not caused by God but sanctioned by him, so free will is carefully respected but finally guidelines for free-will can be established for all time. More on this concept can be found in others of my commentaries (see ww.instituteformerechristianity.org).

Next, the story of Faust, by Goethe, though reminiscent of Job's original, is somewhat different. Goethe's Faust comes to some similar conclusions but uses different terms and different experiences to emphasize his conclusions. We find the same characters; there's God and the accuser, in this case called Mephistopheles. The two make what is termed a wager and Mephistopheles is given free rein to tempt Faust. When the tempter appears, he finds Faust depressed and sullen. Now, Faust is a decent man but he desperately wants answers. What is the meaning of life? What will bring him true happiness? When the Tempter appears, he first conceals his identity and offers to help the depressed Faust. "I can help you find what you're looking for," he boasts, "just become my mentor." Faust is a scientist who searches for answers through rational means. Goethe and Faust lived in the late Eighteenth Century, the period of The Enlightenment, when philosophers eschewed mysticism and used only rationality and logic to seek for answers. Within a hundred and fifty years or so they realized logic could not give a satisfying answer to these questions. That was Faust's predicament, as Goethe, who lived toward the end of the Age of Enlightenment, began to realize. "I'll let you try every possible experience in life. You'll be able to learn for yourself but in the end you'll end up following me," contends Mephistopheles. Well, Faust does come to experience it all: wealth, lust, power, and all human experience. And he comes to a startling conclusion and at the same time, holds on to his positive spiritual attitude about life. Faust comes to realize humans can understand only so much about their lives. There is more to meaning than humans are able to deduce on their own. They don't have the capacity or the tools to discern all. He acknowledges there is something, someone, greater than himself that has a higher perspective. He admits his only moment of true bliss comes from his devotion to and love for Gretchen, a delightful, humble companion he met along the way. And yes, through it all, he is able to distinguish the different shades of moral integrity without succumbing to pure evil for gain as the tempter contends he would.

Similar stories with similar endings have been told. But we don't stop here. The Bible gives us another story. This one is very similar to the Faust story, but this one really happened! The man, like Faust, was a seeker of wisdom and truth. His name was King Solomon, and he lived some three thousand years ago. He, too, sought wisdom and begged God (not Satan) to lead him to profound Understanding of Life. He became renowned for becoming the wisest man of the ancient world. At one point, though, he conducted an experiment very similar to the one Faust, the scientist, proposed and he, Solomon, too utilized himself as the subject of the study. Solomon then went on to attain knowledge and wisdom from all sources, studying naturalistic phenomena and human nature, a social scientist at heart. Not willing to leave any avenue of adventure untried, he experienced every possible aspect of life. Being the king of a Grand Kingdom, he sought to do anything and everything. He actually did what Doctor

Faust was alleged to do in that fictional account. Solomon actually did experience it all. Wealth, power, lust, every whim, every avenue of human experience was explored to find the ultimate satisfaction from all life could offer. He craved what we all crave, Happiness. The difference is he had the means and circumstances to experience all the material world could offer. He followed through on the experiment, unfortunately to his detriment. But fortunately he was able to write down his conclusions for all posterity to read. We don't have to guess and endlessly wonder which pursuits or which avenues of experience might bring true happiness.

King Solomon wrote a full report of his conclusions that are preserved in the Bible book called Ecclesiastes. Toward the beginning of the book, Solomon set down his intentions. Acting as any modern researcher or scientist, he proposed to use empirical evidence, actually living the experiment himself rather than just surmising from intuition, as his method of investigation. Note his plan recorded in Ecclesiastes chapter two and verse three: "I wanted to see what was good for people to do under heaven during the few days of their lives." Then he brags about his accomplishments starting in verse 4 forward: "I undertook great projects: I built houses for myself and planted vineyards…I bought male and female slaves…I amassed silver and gold…a harem as well, the delights of a man's heart." He continues in verse ten: "I denied myself nothing my eyes desired." I'm sure many others have proposed a similar investigation but the big difference is Solomon had the wealth and circumstances to follow through. The idea would be intriguing to many but few, very few, have had the opportunity and life situation to follow through.

Any regular Bible reader realizes the book of Ecclesiastes is very different from the rest of scripture. Solomon gave us a hint as to why. He admits he sought wisdom (all types of wisdom). Certainly, he expected inspiration along the way. But to complete his once in a lifetime (more like once in many millions of lifetime opportunities), he was forced to write devoid of feeling and as dispassionately as possible. He attempted to be totally objective. This is the method scientists and researchers employ today, simple logic and the rational way. All other Bible books put God at the center, and though they write about heart wrenching suffering and humanity at its worst, they always, always interject the positive hope and faith from inspiration. Solomon did not. He does say, "Yet when I surveyed all that my hands had done…everything was meaningless, a chasing after the wind." Pure logic indicated to him men and animals have exactly the same fate, they both die and turn to dust. He repeats over and over the conclusions he reached through human reasoning. All is vanity, Life is meaningless, and that's it. Not one of those pleasures or acquisitions could bring him lasting satisfaction.

Even when it comes to career success, he carefully observed that there was no set formula he could find to offer as a road guide. His assessment, "The race is not to the swift or the battle to the strong… but time and chance happen to them all." One just can't count on anything to be absolutely certain, in life there are too many variables. For example, most well-known actors or actresses will admit they often just happened to be in the right place at the right time. Maybe they were born into a successful family or happened just to be picked at an audition where any one of the many could have gotten the part having had as much or more talent. Life isn't fair, Solomon observed over and over.

From the empirical evidence, Solomon did make a significant contribution to the literature on finding happiness. As we've seen so far, human wisdom doesn't give us much to work with when it comes to finding happiness. The best you can expect, if this life is all there is, "Go eat your food with gladness and drink your wine with a joyful heart… Enjoy life with your wife, whom you love, all the days of this meaningless life that God has given you under the sun." There is some good advice here if you can pass over the depressing, "meaningless" interjection. Solomon learned the important lesson on striving to live in the present. We can't know or control the future. Enjoy what you have, take delight in all the blessings you have in the moment. Don't waste time worrying about the other guy or gal, what they have or what you don't. Life does offer many blessings to most everyone, really enjoy them while you can and in the moment. So often people go through life, never stopping to be sincerely thankful for what they have.

Now for his all-important final conclusion, based on the facts and given the limited understanding and limited capabilities of the human mind. At the end of the book (Eccl. 12:13), "Now all has been heard. Here is the conclusion of the matter: Fear God and keep his commandments, for this is the duty of all mankind… and a judgement". Almost as a belated thought and as though with no alternative, Solomon brings God back into the picture. What he concludes, based on what researchers would call anecdotal evidence, is a rational conclusion. He could console himself to assert, not in so many words but implied, "At least I proved what doesn't bring happiness. I'm at a loss rationally, I've come up to a dead-end. I would have to conclude that having God in one's life is of prime importance. The only area of study I didn't follow-through on in any detail is this spiritual avenue." His biography elsewhere in scripture relates how he started out taking that spiritual path. He begged for Wisdom, and it came in abundance. Unfortunately, he started to rely on those abilities rather than the inspiration that takes one out of the realm of the material to a higher level.

We are indebted to King Solomon. There are many important lessons to be learned from the Job-Solomon-Faust stories. If nothing more take these two with you as keepers: The evidence is clearly summarized by Solomon declaring, "All is meaningless, vanity." Physical pleasure and material possessions can never bring long-term meaning and purpose in life. And second, however, Solomon did hint at the one possibility that he didn't explore rationally in his treatise. That possibility, "Fear the true God," he asserts. Only if there is an omnipotent God is meaning and purpose in life possible. How to react to that directive and how to interpret the term "Fear God" is explained in the rest of the Bible. Thank you, to Solomon, for at least being truthful. He could have bragged about all the momentary joys experienced during a short-lived existence. He could also have made it appear, as so many celebrities attempt, that a life of glamour and notoriety is a life to be envied. No, Solomon affirmed, life is meaningless, vanity…unless we go past the material and sensual pleasures that over time become cloying. The direction given in the end, "Fear the true God and keep his Commands," is a launching point. But that's a topic in itself that takes a whole lifetime to explore and comprehend.

Chapter 6

Happy Ever After

I read an interesting article rather recently that was quite surprising. Researchers often do studies on the idea of "Happiness." They track how the perception of our own happiness level may change over time. Numerous studies have shown, for instance, that in general in the United States the population is not as happy as they were fifty years ago. The reasons are probably obvious to most of us. But this is what is especially fascinating in some recent studies with results totally unexpected. When sociologists carry out surveys in African countries where the population lives in extreme poverty, they discover the level of population happiness on average is higher than the average in America. I know that seems unbelievable. I find this hard to believe myself but the research methodology appears accurate. Apparently these seemingly destitute people may have something to teach our society which may be far advanced technologically but found wanting in what we desire most, happiness.

Wouldn't you like to know what their secret of happiness is? What about the secret of the happiest of past, diverse civilizations?

The fact that our relatives living a hundred years ago, living when the average person survived to the ripe old age of about 50 years yet suffered from diseases routinely cured today, where mothers often died during childbirth and their children often died prematurely, yet were still quite happy, seems to be amazing. I've often pondered "What are we missing?" Long ago I began a personal search for answers. Fortunately during those years I personally had been quite happy with my life as it unfolded, happy enough that, not infrequently, I found myself feeling guilty. I'd exclaim to myself, "Is this fair? I'm so happy and people around the world are starving, why am I so lucky?" Years later when I heard of the third world country studies, I was relieved a bit. All this time, though, I made a quest for the secret of happiness (I didn't even know my own secret!). Being a Christian, I knew that this had something to do with my own high happiness level. I have discovered by following Simple, Practical Christian principles happiness level soared. But that didn't explain happiness in third world countries. Many of them aren't Christians themselves. But we had to have something in common. One obvious similarity is that they are part of the same human race. And that's not a little thing. There appears to be a mechanism within all humans that gives us the capacity to be happy and that's something we can be grateful for and can't be taken for granted. But guess what? I found something else all of us happy people have in common, at least in my estimation. But before I give my thoughts, please take just a moment to consider in your own personal estimation what you think that secret might be…

The simple answer I found was confirmed by the Bible millennia ago, but you don't need a Bible to confirm personal experience. However, I want you to read a couple Bible verses to assure you these aren't just my ideas but for thousands of years the secret has been well enunciated, though most of our ancestors knew it intuitively, just like our third world friends appear to. The simple answer, the secret, in my opinion, is one word…THANKFULNESS. What I'm suggesting is not the perfunctory "thank you" we're taught as a child. What I mean is the kind of "thank you" you say if you've lost your sight and a doctor gives it back to you. How would you say "thank you" then? That's the kind of thankfulness I'm talking about.

To give credence to what I'm suggesting let me relate several verses that helped me crystallize what I believe about happiness. They confirm my personal experience with happiness and are found in the Bible at Colossians chapters 3: 20 to 4:2. The setting was St. Paul, a follower of Jesus, writing his friends in the city of Colossae to offer them some final advice. In so many words he was proclaiming, "I'll not see you again but always remember these last words from me." Notice the word he repeats 3 times. "Let the peace of God rule in your hearts…and be THANKFUL. (3:15) whatever you do, whether in word or deed, do it all in the name of the Lord, Jesus, giving THANKS to God. (3:17) devote yourselves to prayer being watchful and THANKFUL." (4:20) Paul was in effect admonishing, "Go through life giving thanks for whatever happens, whatever you do, whatever your deeds amount to, there will always be something to celebrate there, look for that, be thankful for that. If nothing more, when you have that indescribable "peace of God in your heart" you'll feel at peace with yourself, with God and with your circumstances, stop and appreciate that moment. That is SIMPLE, PRACTICAL CHRISTIANITY. Don't let that precious moment pass you by without acknowledging thanks.

This advice is more appropriate now than ever. With all the sensory overload, the computers, TV and other electronic devices the average person is forced to process billions of pieces of data daily, too much for anyone to meaningfully or humanly process. Stop and focus, even for a moment, on how special life itself is. What a privilege. I was fortunate to relearn the happiness lesson with my son Matthew and now my grandson, Adam. I really did need a refresher course. They forced me to stop and acknowledge the beauty and specialness of sights and sounds they were experiencing for the first time but I was just letting pass me by. All I had to do to enjoy was to take the time.

Here's where the poverty stricken friends we've been talking about have the advantage. They have the time. They don't experience the massive overload that blocks one's senses. They can focus on what's most important, being alive, being surrounded by loving family, and that's the other area where they have an advantage. Community is extremely important where poverty is prevalent. Since community is a source of survival, family and friends are especially dear. Again I stop, reminding myself they have so little and immediately I'm reminded of another paradox of life...the less we have, the more we appreciate. I'm sure you've experienced that like I have. My health is a perfect example. Once upon a time when I thought of myself as having near perfect health I didn't wake up each morning ecstatic and thankful to think I was blessed with another day of vibrant health! Now that I have my own personal set of health issues I do awake each day feeling blessed and thankful for a measure of health. And when I go for a walk each day among the birds and trees you'd better believe I do exclaim, "Thank you!" At one time I used to run every day, now I can only walk, but I don't dismiss that as insignificant. To me less is more. I may be doing less but enjoying it all the more.

Here's an exercise I did that's guaranteed to raise your "Happiness Quotient." A few years ago when I started over from a low point in life, I initiated what I called my "Happiness List," a list I've added to time after time since then. I started my list by reminding myself of the simple pleasures and incredible joys I'd experienced in the past and wanted to relive again. The first thing I remember saying to myself, "Isn't it wonderful I can start over." That's one of the beauties of life, any day I can exclaim, "I'm going to choose to start over!" I can say, "I've gone through a slew of problems and things can only get better from here. I've got a measure of health, I've got a wonderful supportive family, a few special friends and many more friends with whom I'd enjoy keeping in touch." But more than even that, even when I could only lie in bed recuperating, I realized I had a mind, a mind that had helped me work out a meaningful life for myself, and with that mind I've been able to enunciate what I believe in and why. I realize I've got more to do before my time runs out. I've got projects, hopes and dreams waiting to be fulfilled. I came up with the phrase," An Attitude of Gratitude," as a reminder.

One other thing I've taught myself to do each morning on awakening is to remind myself what happened yesterday that I'm thankful for. For example, yesterday I was able to complete some of the research work for an important project, I was able to take a long walk in the sun, I finally got a chance to talk to my brother Mark on the phone and he's well, Marlene made a fantastic dinner (it was just mac & cheese, just wonderful). I've often averred, to me the most special days are the most un-special days. I hope you can understand what I mean. An average day may at first appear to be anything but special but once I'm attune to what's happening around me, the day is transformed into a most special day. I learned once with my son Matt at age 2 to look through the wonderment in his eyes at a new color, a new shape, a new word. I almost forgot but now have a new opportunity with my grandson, Adam, to be dazzled by new sound, brand new colors. I'm relearning the lesson of being thankful for the little things.

The tendency is to think of such a simple lesson as being less than profound. From my perspective the seemingly inconsequential and self-evident truths are really the most profound. The wisest or simplest, the richest or the poorest have no advantages here. As we've seen, our poorest fellow humans in third world countries seem to have grasped the secret of happiness rooted in the act of thankfulness more readily than some of us have. A similar phenomenon appears to be at work in the dynamics with the seemingly wisest of men who are so busy searching meaning way out there somewhere when meaning might be close at hand. As many of you know, the paradox is presented in scripture at Matthew 11:25 where Jesus remarked, "I praise you Father…because you've hidden these things from the wise and learned, and revealed them to little children." The principal expounded here is that the simple ideas that even children can comprehend are the most meaningful. This is the SIMPLE, PRACTICAL CHRISTIANITY I keeping exclaiming over. Less is more and by extension the simple things when appreciated bring true joy.

Now to put it all in perspective. I personally hypothesize that thankfulness is one of the primary ingredients of happiness. How else can we explain why rich or poor, wise or dunce, even Christian or Non-Christian have no special privilege when it comes to happiness. As members of the human race we are all endowed with the ability to find happiness and that in itself is something not to be taken for granted. I believe being able to find meaning in life itself is a capability humans can also be especially thankful for. Meaningfulness coupled with thankfulness can lead to the pinnacle of happiness. I'm hoping you feel resolved to increase your own happiness quotient by being aware of the little things you come across in life that can make you ecstatically happy. Remember "AN ATTITUDE OF GRADITUDE."

Chapter 7

Why I'm A Christian

I'm a Christian. I don't know what kind of connotation that evokes in you, but I think it will be worth hearing my explanation of why I'm a Christian. I'd like you to know how my personal research, reasoning and meditations have led me to the conclusion that for me Christianity is the best choice of WORLD-VIEW. I'm attempting to present a non-threatening explanation which is, of course, my viewpoint. I am not attempting to convert anyone to Christianity here. However, due to the overwhelming negative publicity Christians seem to be getting recently I feel it necessary to provide this alternate take. At the outset, I appeal to your reasonableness to hear, without prejudgment, a simple explanation that I feel is compelling.

First, realize there are more than two billion people now living claiming to be Christian. Probably no two would explain in exactly the same way what it means to be a Christian. That's because every one of us has had a different life experience and a different perspective. However, there are at least three ideas that are both minimally acceptable to all who are Christians and that may be unique to Christianity. These three ideas are the only three I'd like to discuss. Christians all believe there is a higher power that most picture as a personage, a 'God', if you will. They also believe that Jesus as the son of God gave up his life as a sacrifice to benefit all those that avail themselves of his magnanimity. Finally, they all recognize the obligation to show love to others. The Christian perception of these three ideas are somewhat unique to Christianity. For example, some religions, like Hindus, Buddhists and Taoists do not believe in a personal God. And while many religions like Islam believe Jesus was a prophet from God, only Christians give Jesus a special place in their historical records. Finally, while I advocate for Christianity as a helping community, I am talking about a Christianity that is not extreme. Mirroring in the general population, approximately ten percent of the population are extreme conservatives and approximate ten per cent are extreme liberals, that is true of religious institutions in general too. I am not an advocate of Fundamentalist Christians who prefer to interpret Bible wording to be taken literally, like Hell being a literal burning fire, nor do I side with the extreme liberal camp of followers who believe they can believe and do whatever they like as long as their actions do not hurt another at the moment, regardless of long-term ramifications. I would like to think about eighty percent of Christians are putting some effort toward supporting the two main tenets of Christianity per Jesus of Loving God and loving neighbor as self. (Matthew 22:1) Those are the ones I have in mind here.

In the spirit of my thesis as to why I am a Christian I must acknowledge that most religions believe in a morality that is very similar. Note that Two thirds of the world, Christians, Islam and Judaism all essentially believe in the Ten Commandment and even five out of the Ten Commandments (minus the five that mention a personal God) are found almost word for word in Buddhist literature. I applaud all individuals, religious or not, seeking to make our world a better place for humanity. However, since all religions like all political parties are run by humans, both those sincere and those out for personal prominence, we find unethical behavior evident. Since I want to be in fellowship with others attempting to live a life that makes a positive difference and since religions, in general, do far more than any other organizations (including governments) in giving monetary support and volunteer labor for good, I support various religious charities. What I want to do here is analyze these three ideas with the perspective I have arrived at. I beg you not to go ahead of me and draw conclusions before listening to my reasoning. There is wide latitude even within those three issues. For example, I know committed Christians who live as close to the concept of sainthood as you could imagine, but whose views and picture of God are diametrically different, anywhere between viewing God as the wizard in the Wizard of Oz, a little old man who sits behind a giant computer screen and a conglomeration of buttons and knobs keeping order in the universe, to the other extreme of God not being a person but the universe itself as a whole.

Some Christians see God as a spiritual force found anywhere and everywhere in creation, a person, yes, in the sense of intelligence, feeling and goal-orientation. Christian views run the gamut between those extremes. Let's not debate these fine points now, they are a life's project in themselves. Doctrine is not what we are debating here. Doctrine is in fashion and out of fashion but some things do not change. I am asserting from personal experience, through good times and bad, through success and failure, as a single young man, family man and in old age I can recommend the life principle of Christianity. I have spent a lifetime studying the Life principles of many religions and there are beautiful ideas in each. And while I do not admit having all the answers I have studied Christianity at a level few students would ever care to, I can claim I have something special to offer here. I would like you to understand why what I have come to learn as basics of three major issues in Christianity are worth considering. They are an eternal God or "Mighty One" as the original language of Christian scripture asserts. Also, Christianity asserts that Jesus is the Son of God whose mandate was to die for all who might and will ever need that sacrifice to give them the psychological courage to move on with life. Finally, Christianity asserts that the only way one can ever be truly happy is to come to the point where one can put others' interests one a par with one's own welfare. In other words, show "love" to others following the example Jesus set (His Love directive goes further than many religions mandate). That's all, I'm asking you to consider them with me.

WHAT DO YOU MEAN BY "GOD?"

I remember when I was just a young kid interested in science. I loved reading about space, physics and astronomy. I remember so well almost every book I picked up on the subject in the late 60's and early 70's had a question or two about the debate going on among astronomers. Did the universe have a beginning, (the Big Bang Theory) or was the universe always in existence, (the Steady-State Theory). I recall at the time thinking this was such an interesting issue since it brought the theologians into the debate whether they liked it or not. Christianity and the Bible are both very adamant on the topic asserting the universe had a beginning, the first words of the Bible being, "In the beginning..." I listened attentively over the next few years to the debate and the attendant research that was given to support a particular viewpoint. This continued for a number of years until astronomers were able to prove beyond any reasonable doubt that the universe did have a beginning. I remember thinking to myself, with little fanfare, "Well, score one for Christianity."

Further, if I were to believe that all there is in the universe is physical, material elements then I'd have to believe my thoughts are products of physical chemical reactions. That would call into question how I could possibly trust those chemical reactions to lead to valid reasoning. I asked myself and I have to ask anyone, Am I (or are you) prepared to accept the premise that the seemingly logical reasoning that I (or you) are now engaged in is simply material chemical reactions in the brain? Especially when I can easily accept the premise that "thoughts" are non-material, no different than the concept of a non-material God? I wasn't. That's an extreme, unverifiable premise that would take an awful lot more faith to believe than belief in the existence of a non-material world beyond the physical! A non-material component to the universe easily can account for valid reasoning power.

Having a concern for the welfare of others and myself, I began to reason this way. If I have a sense of yearning for true justice, global kindness, and relief from suffering, permanent truth and stability in a changing chaotic world (and I have to admit these are universal desires), then there is only one source conceivably able to rectify our dilemma, an Almighty God, a God beyond the unstable material world. In other words, why would these universe desires persist with no means to fulfill them? I could only conceive of one possible way these yearnings could become a reality, An Almighty God. However, a person must admit the possibility of a world above the physical plane to accept the concept of God. I was willing to admit that.

Furthermore, it's only with a belief in a god who is the epitome of justice and love could I dare to dream that justice and altruism will ever prevail. The Bible even claims "God is Love." Some way some-how wrongs will be righted and some way somehow every human will know what it means to be loved for no other reason than that he or she is a fellow being. These are noble dreams that can only be envisioned in conjunction with the concept of a God of Love. I realize this is not a proof of the existence of God. Philosophically it's impossible to prove a position beyond all doubt. But belief in God is the only alternative that allows for these majestic dreams to possibly come true.

I realized, too, one of the other benefits of belief in a God. Psychologists insist that stress and a frantic lifestyle take their toll on health. Yet belief in a benevolent Higher Power helps diffuse some of life's chaos. Also we're advised that an attitude of optimism is benefi-cial for both mental and physical wellbeing, the more optimistic the outlook the less tendency toward depression. Here again credence in a benevolent God promotes an air of optimism. To feel you're bob-bing in an ocean with no sense of control is a horrible sensation. To feel there is no control over how you're treated is extremely enervat-ing. I didn't want to live that way. Furthermore, psychologists concur that stability and absence of worry about one's right to human dig-nity are key for a fully functioning life. Yet I'd contend such order can't even be conceived without confidence in a higher power. The belief in an engaged God promotes confidence in a life that is not all chance but has the element of stability. There are so many benefits that come with belief in a God, and since neither alternative can be proved logically beyond doubt, I'd be foolish to reject the one alter-native (belief in God) that offers so many immediate benefits.

About the same time as I was contemplating the evidence for a higher power from physical science and logic, I was beginning my studies in psychology and sociology. I found to my bewilderment hot debates over other issues that were in some way connected to Christianity, issues where Christianity had a vested interest in seeing resolved. Issues, such as family values, were of major concern. Many of my mentors in sociology were suggesting that Family, a traditional societal norm, would soon be a thing of the past. They were certain that research would soon show that traditional family settings were not necessary or would have no affect on success of raising children. I remember when a well-known sociologist was all but boycotted and pilloried for having the audacity to print his research showing one of the major contributors to the growing disenfranchisement of inner-city populations was the startling increase of single parent families in those inner cities. This was the first time I heard the term, "politically incorrect" and was indignant to find that the powers that be would not allow data and research on this branch of family studies to be published in reputable academic journals. It was too volatile a topic. Eventually, as other research and data over the next decade would trickle in, it became very clear to all that a traditional family environment was by far the most successful venue for providing well-adjusted, productive members of society. Though many sociologists objected, stating the data only proves that the traditional family is still the most successful means of socializing children but that it did not prove it is the only means. To date, these objectors have not suggested an alternative that has long-term data to recommend its veracity. Again, though it took 10 or 15 years for this positive family data to surface, I said to myself with little fanfare, "Another point for Christianity!"

Time after time I found that my fields of study (sociology and psychology) had published tomes of data indirectly verifying that Christian principles have a place in our modern world. Here I mention just one example. A field of particular interest in my research has been self-help psychology. I have been around to observe the ebb and flow of the popularity of the field. The basic thread running through all the research and volumes on this topic is the importance of using the conscious and subconscious mind to effect change in a person's self and the world around him or her. Whether the advice is on imaging or goal setting or the current fad, especially in business, of using intuition to usher in success, these data which include both rigorous scientific studies and also compelling anecdotal data confirms the Christian principle of the power of the mind. Writers will often quote the much-repeated Biblical assertion, "As a man thinketh so shall he be ....." and other biblical aphorisms on the power of the mind, usually without giving any credit to the original source of the profound idea. The discoveries of these principles associated with healthy, successful living are extolled with no reference to any antecedent Christian source. Again, as the data came in I have simply mused, "Another point on the side for the veracity of Christianity!"

So, this is my thesis. Since time after time studies confirm the practicality of Christian principles for living and there have been, to my knowledge, no proven errors in the Christian philosophy for 2000 years, I have to conclude that Christian values are relevant. Sure, many psychologists disagree with scripture, but actual research studies do not confirm their speculation. A perfect example is family life. The Bible asserts that a family with husband and wife is the best vehicle for raising children. Many psychologists retort from that claim and put the onus on poverty yet year after year the statistics of children and one parent families prove otherwise. (This is not the place to discuss this in detail though). Since Christian principles have remained stable for these millennia, the probability of their future relevance is very strong.

Not long ago I was sitting in a research seminar when several sociologists who were not Christians were reporting on the results of studies on non-localized prayer, the evidence showing that prayer by Christians, even when the person being prayed for doesn't realize someone is praying for him, will have a statistically significant effect on his recovery. If time after time, the group of subjects being prayed for (without them or the doctors and nursing staff even knowing prayer is being used) show a statistically significant favorable recovery compared to the non-prayed for group, there is no other known explanation for this. The only possible interpretation is that there are powers beyond physical powers allowed for in a purely material world. When some in the audience became indignant that the data was being reported, the researcher responded, "Don't blame me, I'm just repeating the results. I'm as surprised as you are with the results. I can't explain it, but my ethics force me to report the facts." Rather than immediately objecting to data because the results tend to support Christian doctrine, I feel any seeker of truth would conclude that this is another case where Christianity has an uncanny record of having its claims verified by scientific studies. I've had to admit the further we venture into a scientific world, the evidence piles up to support Christian principles. In every case I've researched of discrepant assertions, it's always based on hearsay or taking statements from the Bible out of context. Rationally, I have been led to admit the Christian principles of living are true and since the source claims to be that of a higher power, I can find no rational reason to refute the claim. This, of course, is not absolute proof but that in fact is what Christian Biblical writings dare us to do, "Test me in this, says the Lord Almighty…" (Malachi 3:10 in the Bible). There is always a necessity for faith. Belief in any philosophy requires faith but when evidence repeatedly piles up to confirm the assertions of Christian faith, I have found the initial need for faith to be the most reasonable conclusion.

So, when I read that Christianity is based on the idea that there is a higher power who created the universe "in the beginning" and he chose to provide tenets for living that have stood the test of time and the vigorous research by our scientific community, I marvel and am humbled to admit the evidence points to there being a higher power or God as Christianity claims. I accept this on faith just as any secular religion like communism, atheism or agnosticism requires acceptance on faith. I, at least, have reams of data and research I can point to that has led me in the direction of the Christian faith.

As I have lived as a Christian I have been amazed to find (though I shouldn't be amazed) that the experiences and successes of my personal life and my personal walk with the God that I originally had to accept based on faith, has been confirmed. Again, you'll say, "Well, that's your personal interpretation", and I have to admit, "Yes, it is." But I would appeal to you by asking, why it is that the vast majority (scientific probability, again) of people, who take the 'leap of faith' that the nineteenth century philosopher Kierkegaard recommended, have overwhelmingly testified it has worked in their lives? They have gotten personal evidence, personal experience that occurs in their lives too often to explain away as chance, continually confirming there is a God and that he cares about us. That's why I have faith in the God of Christianity. Again, who this God is, what type of entity He is, can be interpreted in many different ways by different Christian groups. But there is a Higher Power. Let's not get bogged down with semantic terms like "all powerful, all knowing" when you as a neophyte Christian can accept the minimal belief in a God, a higher power, existing before the beginning, as reasonably evident.

JESUS' SACRIFICE

The major assertion that separates Christians from other religious or spiritual seekers is the belief that Jesus gave up his life as a sacrifice for the benefit of all who believe in him. My purpose here is not to discuss the issue from a theological standpoint but merely from a logical view. This is a rather esoteric concept and may, for some, require further Biblical references. My goal here is to pass on the excitement I feel that modern scientific research is proving the value of this Christian principle (not so much a doctrine but a principle for living).

The issue here is the issue of forgiveness. In my studies and work in the field of social psychology, I frequently encounter the necessity for personal forgiveness. Fortunately, modern psychology has produced an avalanche of data demonstrating that individuals have a difficult time coping with relationships and attaining personal self-esteem without being able to forgive others or themselves for past transgressions. We now understand that an individual may not be able to grow emotionally and in self-concept if he is stifled by an inability to forgive others or self. Countless studies show that an individual may have every right to disparage and castigate another for a heinous offense against him, but if that individual is not able to go beyond that hatred of the offender, he's unable to move on with his own life. He inadvertently hurts himself. Personal growth, emotional growth, is affected adversely. This is especially true if an individual is not able to forgive herself for past actions. What she may have done may appear so horrible to her that no amount of therapy will convince her to forgive herself. Remember, I'm talking strictly from a social scientific standpoint here. These data are verified by rigorous research. Unless a person is able to reach the point of forgiveness, they cannot forget. If she cannot forget, that equates to carrying around harmful baggage that prevents nimble self-maneuvering in daily life. I've tried to convince others, when I've engaged in counseling, to simply 'let it go' but they can't. Imagine struggling with a person who has for years never let himself forget, that due to past inability as a parent, his son committed suicide. Or what do you say to someone who, in a fit of anger, murdered his best friend? Psychologists can work for years with such a patient convinced that they have all but coaxed the patient to move on, only to find that they relapse into total disintegration. What can you say? Have you ever had some part of your past life come back to haunt you, something you aren't proud of and something others won't let you forget? Psychologists will tell you such a situation can be very difficult to resolve. And yet, resolve it the patient must, if he is to grow. I'm not going to belabor the point of importance of self-concept and self-esteem here. I trust most all will concede the critical need of a positive self-concept to be fully functioning.

Happily, one concept that works, I have found, and works consistently, is an appeal to the Christian concept of Jesus' sacrifice. I find this appeal will work for anyone, regardless of a person's own personal religious persuasion. Again, my goal here is to explain the concept without evoking a debate over whether Jesus is the Son of God or even what it means to claim Jesus is the Son of God. One's own convictions come with further meditation and soul searching. Note, this is what Christianity can offer that few other religions can offer. Jesus, the Christ, in effect proclaimed, "I am willing to go through unspeakable suffering, martyrdom, death, to be punished for something I didn't do. And I'm willing to do this for you. I'm going to be subjected to inhuman torture and death because I'm not willing to deny truth. That's my only crime, not being willing to renounce truth and to keep quiet, nothing more." How many other martyrs have experienced a similar fate, from Biblical prophets to political martyrs even in our time? What happened to Jesus has been repeated countless times. We are all familiar with that. So it's not difficult to accept that such a fate occurred to Jesus. In fact, his followers after Jesus' death were willing to undergo the same fate rather than deny what they had personally witnessed. No more convincing proof need be offered of any event occurring then that the witnesses to the event are willing to die themselves rather than deny the facts of the event.

But here's the point of this sacrifice. Jesus said, "I am willing to suffer for you, be punished for you, tortured for you, and die for you. I am willing to do this of my own volition so you can have this priceless feeling of forgiveness for yourself and as an inducement for you to forgive others." When you feel, for example, that you committed an unspeakable crime, caused another person to suffer, did something you are extremely ashamed of, follow Jesus' advice. Jesus, in effect, said, "Ask yourself what is the worst punishment you could imagine for your crime or culpable action? Do you feel you deserve to be tortured, to undergo a slow methodical torture of unspeakable pain and torment that eventually leads to death?" Most of us would be willing to concede that such a personal ordeal might be enough to expiate one's past transgressions. However, most of us lack the courage and conviction to undergo such a punishment. Jesus said, "No matter. You don't have to subject yourselves to such agony, I did it for you! So whenever you feel despair and beyond consolation and dejected, just consciously apply my agony for your agony. Don't waste what I did. Please apply it to yourself, for yourself! I've undergone the most ignominious suffering for you freely and without coercion. So when you feel you should be punished or need to atone for your errors, apply my personal suffering for yourself. I only ask that you ask forgiveness for what you've done, apply my punishment for what you think you might deserve and resolve to try to do better the next time. And then be willing to forgive still others. Remember, I am willing to apply my punishment on your behalf for whatever recompense you feel you deserve."

This concept really works! I've had real success using this concept in my personal counseling. Furthermore, countless millions throughout history have been able to start new lives without years of therapy by first understanding the concept and being willing to impute this act of Jesus for themselves. No other religion has such a powerful concept that can be used practically, efficiently and successfully. Other religions or non- theological therapies attempt to say, "You should forgive yourself, God loves you or it wasn't so bad what you did and I think you should forgive yourself." But only one world view offers such a reasonable, easily understood concept to effect forgiveness. This is the beauty of Christianity. It's practical, it works. And note, I did not appeal to the claim that Jesus is the Son of God and what that adds to the equation. There is no need to argue that issue here. It's a matter each can individually deal with once he understands the believable, reasonable basis for being able to start a new life. I'm proud to be a Christian due to the simplicity and beauty of this solely Christian doctrine of sacrifice!

<u>LOVE IS NOT A TRITE IDEA</u>

The third aspect of Christian doctrine that I wish to explore is the directive to show love to others. I must first say this is no longer a uniquely Christian practice. Those living through the 1970's remember when psychologists and the popular media (music, books, etc.) touted the beauty of this lifestyle and the importance of love as a necessity for psychological well adjustment. This was a Christian concept central to Christianity and stressed by Christianity more so than any other world religion. The data in the Twentieth Century on the preeminence of "love" was so powerful it was immediately taken up but never was equated with the essence of the Christian teaching. The revelations on love made thousands of psychologists popular and effective in therapy without any deference to Christianity. I'm saying, a conspicuous oversight of this celebration of love was that credit was seldom given to Christianity as the original source of this idea. Psychologists began to present a great deal of scientific research proving the benefits to all parties from a display of true love. Countless studies verify that benefactors of love are rewarded with psychological, emotional and physiological benefits themselves. Research, however, was presented as if these were original discoveries without stating they were a restatement and verification of Judeo – Christian doctrine. Unfortunately, the 'importance of love' has become a trite phrase with much of the power of the Biblical directive emasculated.

The other note I hasten to make about the uniquely Christian doctrine of love is the positive connotation given to the biblical directive to love. Love means 'doing unto others', 'showing love', in an active rather than merely reactive way. It is far more than refraining from harming but includes the aspect of initiating action with the motive of benefiting others. Christian love is not the idea of 'do not do unto others as you would not have them do unto you,' which is a passive restatement of the Golden Rule taught in some other religions. Further, other religions may acknowledge the importance of love in their dogma but never to the extent Christianity does. Christians believe 'God is love' or the epitome of love. The contrast is quite clear when one compares the squalor and suffering in third-world, non-Christian countries whose cultures were originally based on non-Christian passive love, to the conditions in countries whose laws were traditionally based on Judeo-Christian guidelines. Of course, nominal Christian countries have not totally eradicated physical suffering but have at least made an appreciable dent in it compared to non-Christian countries. Of course, communist countries have accomplished similar feats but only with concomitant loss of freedom. Please realize I am not asserting this to start a debate to which one might take exception but only to illustrate what I mean by "active love" versus "passive love".

I also should add that Christian Biblical writings never do give an actual definition of love. The best that it does is to either give examples of what love (the Bible uses the Greek word, "agape", rather than simply "philos" which is 'brotherly love') is like; for example, the freely given sacrifice of Jesus' own life or the unselfish sharing of physical needs by early Christians even when they had barely enough to survive themselves. The Bible also in attempting to illustrate the magnitude of true love gives an elaborate list of what love is 'not'. The apostle Paul said love,"does not envy, does not boast, and is not proud, not rude, not self-seeking, not easily angered, keeps any record of wrongs. Love does not delight in evil but rejoices with the truth." (1 Corinthians 13:4-6 in the Bible) Recognizing that any definition of love only serves to limit the magnitude of its value, I still like to say, "Love is an unselfish concern for others backed by positive action to help, but much more." When I hear of the 'good' being done in the name of love and the positive contributions to humanity of countless present and past Christians like Mother Theresa, I'm humbled and proud to be a Christian.

MY CONCLUSIONS

Let me say it again, I'm proud to be a Christian. I daily reap the benefits of being a Christian. Three major tenets of Christian doctrine (there may be more but these three are shared by all who claim to be Christians) give me a starting point or foundation from which to build my life. I believe in a God, a higher power, that is the reference point for all reality. This source, as science has shown, is the beginning of all reality and therefore is the reference point from which all reality can be gauged. Knowing that life was shared with me or that I am one of the products of the universal beginning, I am not without direction for my life.

The universe is expanding, there are endless opportunities. That's a basis for optimism, hope for the future, a better world. This, in fact, is the spirit of Christianity – a spirit of optimism, always recognizing improvement is possible, improvement for my society, improvement for me and those around me. That makes life exciting and interesting. I fervently hope you, too, can catch the excitement of Christianity. As Jesus said, "All things are possible for those who believe". (Mark 9:23 in the Bible) This is another discovery of modern psychology that has been employed for thousands of years in Christianity and its antecedents. The power of the mind, but that's another chapter to explore in Christian doctrine. I've lived that way for many years. I believe what Jesus said, "All things are possible for those who believe". I've witnessed seeming miracles in my life, countless miracles by insisting on living in a hopeful, optimistic manner.

A Christian recognizes all people live by faith. We all make assumptions about life and live based on those assumptions. We can assume life has arisen from nothingness (of course, you have to admit there was a beginning from all the scientific evidence) and will progress (again, that's an assumption of most atheists too, that we can make progress) but based only on where chemical reactions, not divine intelligence, can lead us. But somehow intelligence has, by chance, surfaced in the universe, so we can have "faith" that a positive future is possible. That takes an awful lot of faith in my estimation. The other alternative takes faith too, but in my estimation, far less blind faith. We know the universe and life had a beginning, we know life shows evidence of intelligent design. The step to believe in a higher power takes faith, but nowhere near the faith needed, in my view, to believe in the power of chemicals and chemical reactions. We know that recent social scientific research has affirmed repeatedly the traditional values associated with a belief in a higher power. The importance for social well being of love, forgiveness, optimism, goal-orientation, grounding in values have not been diminished but affirmed. All these confirmations make it much easier to take the Christian "Leap of Faith" rather than the "chemical reaction" "Leap of Faith."

Once, as a young man, I was naïve enough to accept the challenge of the Biblical prophet who claimed to speak from God, "Test me in this, says the Lord Almighty, and see if I will not throw open the floodgates of heaven and pour out so much blessing that you will not have room enough for it." (Malachi 3:10 in the Bible). I took the challenge; I tested the Christian way of life. It's all come to pass beyond my fondest expectations. The wishes, the dreams, the hopes and an exciting, stimulating life have followed. I testify to this for several reasons. First, I want to make it clear that though I may have started out with a motive of personal gain, over time I found that motive has subtly been transformed into a concern for others, too. I can predict that if you are in need of something better for your life and you are willing to take my invitation, you will undergo the same transformation I did. Your motive may very well be a seemingly selfish motive of a better life; you'll get that but somewhere down the road you'll notice a subtle change. Once you've been satisfied with the true peace of mind you have always cherished but didn't realize was missing, you'll want to see others satisfied too.

THE CHALLENGE

So, this takes me to the greatest proof of the veracity of the Christian philosophy that I can offer. It works! I realize I've proved it to myself but not to you. I insist, though, your making the effort will prove to be the greatest proof to you. The nineteenth century Danish philosopher called it, "the Leap of Faith". I know that every person who has been a Christian for any appreciable length of time that I've interviewed says the same thing. The greatest proof that there is a God or that Christianity is a meaningful way of life is that it works. Ultimately, the happiness, the peace of mind, the inner-tranquility is my personal proof I've chosen the correct course. I challenge you to take the same challenge I did years ago. "Test me in this, says the Lord Almighty, and see if I will not throw open the floodgates of heaven and pour out so much blessing that you will not have room enough for it." (In the Bible quoted earlier). Christianity is a positive, optimistic World-View with the belief Good will triumph in the end. We need more of that in our world. I'm confident you'll find, as I did, the optimistic promise of Jesus will be confirmed for you that, "All things are possible for those who believe."

Chapter 8

Rethinking The Old Testament

People frequently ask, "How can you equate a God of Love to the Old Testament directive for the Israelites to go into a village, destroy it and kill all including women and children? Many would-be students of the Bible are turned off on further Bible investigation when they cannot get a satisfactory answer. Asking in a slightly different way, "How do you justify Jesus' directive to "Love your enemy" with the Old Testament commands like the one in Deuteronomy 2:34? "At the time we took all his towns and completely destroyed them-men, women and children. We left no survivors." So that there is no question, read 1 Samuel 15:2-3 where Samuel the prophet of God has to say, "This is what the Lord Almighty says, "I will punish the Amalekites…Now go, attack the Amalekites and destroy everything that belongs to them. Do not spare them; put to death men and women, children and infants, sheep and cattle…" They ask, "Can those commands come from the same God? My answer is an unreserved, "NO." Yet I and many others who are Christians believe the Bible as the "word of God." I see no contradiction here as long as we read the Bible the way I believe it needs to be read. Before I explain, let me confess, "I don't have all the answers." No one does. When scholars throughout history interpret scripture, the fact that they find seeming contradictions prove these scholars do not have all the answers and yet many will have you believe their interpretations are beyond second guessing. All I can say as I embark on my attempt to make sense of the apparent contradictions, like the one just sighted, is this. Anyone that claims he has all the answers, including I if I did (but I do not) must be assessed with suspicion. REMEMBER ALWAYS, the Bible may be true and may be "The Word of God" but interpretation of the Bible is prone to error. So, this is how I make sense of these thorny issues. I am going to present several different ways to look at this situation. My goal is to show these directives are not God's instructions but man's understanding of what God expected. The blame is not with God, if anywhere, the blame can be placed with AN ANCIENT SOCIAL RULE ingrained in most cultures and never questioned even to this day. I will explain. I ask readers not to criticize my reasoning until you have read through the different ideas presented that include historical records, Bible verses, sociological discoveries, logical reasoning and ethical principles. Then I ask readers to assess for themselves, after taking these thoughts into consideration, whether there really are contradictions that are justified.

Before we go on, I want to be sure we all agree; at least on the surface there appears to be a dilemma for Christians. I say this because some believers seem to squirm out of this predicament by saying, "I believe that God is a loving and fair Father. There is no issue for me. I maybe cannot explain the dilemma, but I know God is ethical and fair, so I'm not going to worry about any inconsistencies." That's the easy way out. However, it is not the preferred way! Scripture tells us that a Christian should always be able to make a defense for his faith.

A believer's mandate is not just to believe but to witness to others, to help others come to a clear picture of who Jesus is and what the Christian way is. Furthermore, what kind of Christian is one who hears a sincere seeker beg, "I'd like to believe but how can I believe and put my trust in this God of yours who could be so ruthless as to command the slaughter of innocent women and children which are considered "war crimes" in our modern world?" and not feel a responsibility to help him find a reasonable answer. Even the Nazis after World War II were executed for their horrendous massacre of Jews including women and children. Some seekers are saying, "Are you asking me to worship someone portrayed as a bloodthirsty god in the Bible?" Yet some Christians throw up their hands in frustration only to respond, "I'm sorry, either you worship this God of the Bible or you'll be punished regardless of your objections." I appeal to Christians to have mercy on sincere non-believers who are begging for answers so they, too, can believe.

And the answers are not so difficult to understand if one is patient enough to listen to the possible solutions to seeming biblical dilemmas. Let me present to you several possible yet simple ways to make sense out of these issues. First let me comment on the unrealistic and non-answers given by believers over several thousand years. Some claim, "God is creator and giver of life so therefore he can take life away if he wishes to; isn't that fair?" Well, I don't know if such a retort is a worthy answer. Back when I was a little kid, I was taught an act of giving and taking away was wrong and we called such unscrupulous agents "Indian Givers." So that superfluous answer to critics is not much of an argument in favor of belief in any god. I beg of you not to stoop to such a degrading level as to give that kind of answer to a sincere seeker wanting to believe in something so crucial that their lives and future happiness is at stake. That kind of talk is not only a non-answer, but it appears to suggest Christians are "unreasoning robots." I HAVE interjected this paragraph to stress our topic is a critical issue believers cannot gloss over. In fact, one of the reasons I'm writing this article and making such a strong issue about the matter is that I feel many Christians appear to be reluctant to stand up for their faith, that is my impression anyway.

Let us get to our discussion in earnest now. Here is the crux of the matter again. We commence with Deuteronomy 2:34. "At that time we took all his towns and completely destroyed them-men, women and children." How are we to take that statement especially in view of God's words to Moses at the beginning of that chapter. Verse 5 and 6 (before verse 34) of the chapter recounts, "The Lord said to me...Do not provoke them to war, for I will not give you any of their land, not even enough to put your foot on...I have given Esau the hill country...you are to pay them in silver for the food you eat and the water you drink." Note that these verses are a little more like how we would expect God to act, are they not? They also remind us to always read the context of the text for true meaning. When Israel was forced to engage in warfare, the situation had changed. verse 30 says "But Siphon king of Heshbon refused to let us pass through for the Lord had made his spirit stubborn and his spirit abstinent." Now the Israelites were meeting with resistance. This King would not even let them pass through his territory. They had no intention of fighting, no intention of killing women and children. Yet hundreds of thousands of people could not survive in the wilderness for long. They were forced to pass through and if necessary, fight if provoked. Also note the other contradiction here. The Bible tells us God gives us Freewill; God never forces humans to submit to him. Yet the Israelites interpreted King Sihon's obstinance to God being the one making his spirit stubborn. If that were true, that is not freewill, is it?

So, which way is it? I would have to say this contradictory language is warning us to realize Bible characters do not always understand what is really happening. They report accurately what they see but their interpretations may not be accurate.

Finally, to judge the ethics of how Moses directs his people to slaughter the innocent we must read with discernment. The scriptural account states clearly, "The Lord said to me (Moses), "See, I have begun to deliver Sihon and his country over to you" (v.31) and in closing out the account the writer stresses "But in accordance with the command of the Lord our God, you will not encroach on any of the land of the Ammonites, neither the land along the course of the Jabbok nor that around the towns in the hills." So, note before we go on, God is being portrayed as being very discriminating in his treatment of enemies of his people, not meting out the same treatment to all. In addition to reading scripture in context we must also read history in context. The world of three thousand years ago was quite different from our modern world. We must judge how the Israelites acted in context with how warfare was engaged in back then. Recall the standard practice among all societies then was for the victor to either take the conquered into slavery OR to decimate the conquered to the last women and child to assure they could never rise at some future date to again challenge the conquerors. Living in that extreme environment helps explain nations' actions. We will talk more about this later. But the big question is, did the Lord actually say those words about women and children or did Moses assume those destructive words were meant or did Moses assume he was to act based on the custom of the times? Let us examine this in more detail before passing final judgement.

Here is where we bring Jesus himself and the New Testament of Scripture into the conversation. The Hebrew writers made some major assumptions during their interaction with God over the centuries and only much later with Jesus coming he clarified their misconceptions. One assumption those of Old Testament times and many Christians today believe is that God will manipulate humans to act against their personality and character. One of the core Bible teachings is that humans were created with FREEWILL. The Lord never forces them to act against their normal character. Scripture makes it very clear that God is not the author of evil or sin, humans themselves are the culprits. James tells us in no ambiguous terms, "When tempted, no one should say 'God is tempting me.' For God cannot be tempted by evil, nor does he tempt anyone, but each is tempted when, by his own evil desire. he is dragged away and enticed." (James 1:13-14) So when scriptural accounts say that God forced King Sihon to pick a fight with the Israelites, what actually happened is that God maneuvered circumstances so the King would act according to his normal disposition. They assumed that their God caused enemies like King Sihon to pick a fight with His people when in reality God was allowing circumstances to force the King to show his true hand. The King was acting selfishly from his own volition, he needed no coaxing. Similarly, Moses, himself made assumptions about how wars were to be fought. He simply followed the example of other nations in battle, that is my take on the matter. But let's bring in Jesus' own explanation of assumed biblical contradictions. When he came, he had to deal with these often. The Jews of Jesus' day assumed the customs, laws and attitudes of their ancestors were absolute truth when in reality some were merely customs handed down from generation to generation when no one took the authority to state empathetically, "This is wrong!" However, Jesus did take that authority and he did set matters straight numerous times.

We start with this simple example in Matthew chapter 5:31-2. "It has been said, anyone who divorces his wife must give her a certificate of divorce. BUT I TELL YOU anyone who divorces his wife, except for martial unfaithfulness, causes her to become an adulteress..." All the way back to Moses, who delivered the Ten Commandants including this command on divorce, the Jews had been allowed to skirt the pure law with exceptions. Jesus showed this was not what God intended, he ALLOWED but did not intend. There is a big difference. Multiple wives were not God's intention originally, but he allowed the Jews, who observed customs other nations nearby were practicing and felt such practices should be permissible for them, also to follow. In fact, it was Moses who made this concession on divorce Jesus was referring to, not God. I would also contend that it was Moses' interpretation on warfare that permitted the killing of innocent bystanders, from my interpretation of scripture.

As we will find there are several reasonable alternative under-standings (and may be more) to rationalize God's reluctance to insist on purer behavior. The world back then had customs ingrained in the nations for many hundreds of years and the Lord in time would be much more insistent on purer behavior. Traveling into the Promised Land and becoming a nation on their own right, the Jewish leaders back then may have rationalized that since they were told they were God's chosen people, they had no choice but to keep their ethnic lin-eage pure by any means possible. They were told on many occasions not to be contaminated by the immoral tribes they would encounter on their journey. So, when Moses told them to follow the warfare tactics of the other tribes they would encounter, following their war strategies would appear to be logical protocol. Allowing for no survi-vors among those pagan tribes living in close proximity would make sense. But again, this was not the Lord's best choice. It was expedient but not the preferred choice.

So far, we have several logical arguments for why God allowed Israel to practice unethical behavior. For one thing, God appears to be patient with his people. He allowed them to follow many customs common to the world at the time with the intent that purer practices would be instituted later. We suggest that interpretation of God's guidelines may have been aligned in accordance with the practices of the time. And we suggest environmental context played a part in understanding Jewish actions. We'll talk more about this later but the ancient view toward life was much different than our modern world's perspective. Theirs was a much crueler world and life itself was more precarious. A good percentage of families expected to lose at least one child to disease or sickness and often women would die during childbirth. The death of a child or the death of a mother was not at all unexpected, it happened frequently. People lived expecting that life would be much more calamitous than our experience. Given that deaths occurred very frequently and was no surprise, life was much more tentative. For example, in our society an adult dying in his or her forties is considered unexpected and a deep tragedy. However, some now living can remember in the earlier Twentieth Century, the life span of adults was some fifty years. With so many deaths, previous generations were much more inured to the pain of death. So, when we read of women and children involved in mass killings in ancient times it was indeed a tragedy but not at all unanticipated. So many tragic deaths certainly did not make them excusable, but death at young ages was commonplace and therefore not as shocking as now.

There is a crucial understanding we need to acquire to resolve and fully settle the matter of God's connection to a less than moral practice. We should settle whether Moses' instructions to the people were God's actual directives to Moses or were they based on the meditations of Moses? No doubt Moses reasoned this way. "After all, we Israelites are God's chosen people and Yahweh instructed us to continue as a pure nation, not be contaminated by the immoral practices of the heathen settlements round about. The twelve tribes and our ancestors have cherished the promise to them through Abraham for over four hundred years now and this is the time for that promise to be fulfilled. We sued for peace with these pagans and they have refused, in fact, they raised armies to fight us first. We have no choice but to fight back. And for them to respect us we must use the same tactics against them as they would toward us. Furthermore, they are the same tactics Abraham our forefather had to live with. This principle of 'An eye for an eye and a tooth for a tooth,' is the moral practice of our times. We are justified to adhere to the same code." No doubt, this is the reasoning Moses used in his meditations asking the Lord for guidance on how to proceed when his plans to pass through another tribe's territory was thwarted. I would also suggest that it was not the Lord who told Moses to kill women and children but that the above thoughts flooded Moses' mind as he prayed. Moses could then say, based on his own meditations, the Lord "told him what to do." I think many of us have had such an experience ourselves. We pray for an answer to a problem and immediately our minds are filled with ideas and knowing that is the way God often answers prayers, we conclude the Lord is telling us how to act. Consequently, following meditations, Moses proclaimed. "God told me such and such," when in actuality God did not verbally talk to him. I'm quite convinced that is true of Moses on this occasion when he announced to his followers in effect that killing these bystanders was justified. I would anticipate many of us, who have dealt with God before, will agree with my assessment here.

To substantiate this reasoning, consider, the Jews lived by the strict principle of "An eye for an eye" for over a thousand years till the coming of the Messiah. Jesus made it clear that the time had come to analyze this rule observed by His people. This is where the real problem is. Matthew 5:38-9 bears this out, "You have heard it said 'An eye for an eye, and a tooth for a tooth.' But I tell you, do not resist an evil person…" Jesus by this statement called into question this rule observed since Moses' time and before. Later he went on to elaborate the New Command, in place of the ancient and outdated rubric of "an eye for an eye." This New Command to love in imitation of God's Love toward us and this command of love was held up as the true, full picture of what love was intended to be all along. Jesus' love was such that one would die for one's brothers and sisters like Jesus modeled for us with his example of sacrificing his own life for the whole world's benefit. So, we have Jesus' own remarks to substantiate this "Eye for an eye" principal Moses employed, which included the practice of killing babies and mothers, was never God's intention. He allowed but did not initiate the practice. Throughout scripture we find emphasized the Lord will allow his people to act expediently, but when the time was right, He no longer patiently condoned questionable behavior in favor of more perfect actions.

This is probably a convenient place to verify the war practices of the neighboring nations in Judean territories. I happened on this set of verses when reading of the social context the Jews were confronted with. Read 2 Kings 8:12 where Elisha, the prophet, had a conversation with a soon to be enemy of his people. Elisha prophesized to Hazael that he would soon become the king of a competing territory and immediately began weeping. Taking up there, "'Why is my lord weeping?' asked Hazael. 'Because I know the harm you will do to the Israelites,' he answered. 'You will set fire to their fortified place, kill their young men with the sword, dash their children to the ground and rip open their pregnant women.'" From here, the expectations of war battles were quite clear. Elisha knew as soon as he saw Hazael he could immediately predict by his first impression; this man was evil. Though he appeared to be a personable and considerate man, his demeanor belied the fact he was no different than all other men seeking power. He would follow the same practices of the other kings of the time, slaying men, women and children indiscriminately. The Jews followed the same procedure familiar to their forefather, Abraham. This was, in turn, a pattern first observed by Abraham's own father from his native birthplace of Ur of the Chaldeans, "An eye for an eye." Even to this very day, we have remnants of the actual Code of Hammurabi in writing containing those very words, words the Israelites lived by written hundreds of years before Abraham's time, some four thousand years ago. This was the law of the land and therefore the Israelites adopted it, transferred from custom before writing was invented to Hammurabi to Abraham to Moses to David and all the way down to the time of Jesus. In fact, to this day many of the descendants of Abraham, specifically the modern nation of Israel and all the Moslem nations, billions of people, still live by that code. This rubric, accepted as a rule of justice in ancient times without anyone questioning its consequences, and accepted by many today as a way to ensure justice prevails, actually ensures Injustice, as we will explain later!

What we are demonstrating is in the ancient world the "Eye for Eye" mentality was ingrained in the minds of most of the world's inhabitants. Moses, too, grew up during that time period. So, we return to the question posed earlier. When Moses stated God told him how to treat their conquered peoples, he, rather than hearing a voice from God directly, as he had heard on the occasion of the "Burning Bush," he simply sensed how he was to handle those conquered ones, the rule was clear and had been followed by the ancient world for over a thousand year before Moses' time. I firmly believe Moses' experience here was of this later sort. Quite often in scripture we read of the prophets having spoken or communicated with God when in deep meditation and prayer using the same wording as Moses. On one occasion, for example, Jeremiah describes his encounter with God this way, "The word of the Lord came to me," (Jeremiah 1:4) not in actual spoken words out loud but in his meditations. From personal experience, as I've commented, when I have prayed for guidance and an answer "pops into my head" before the prayer is finished, I chock it up to intuition and even inspiration. I say, as others do, "God told me this is what I'm to do." It appears to me in the same way the prophets and Moses similarly described their encounters with God. Even after Jesus left earth, the Apostle Peter tells us of his experience of inspiration in a dream which moved him to start thinking about how Jewish Christians were to view non-Jewish believers, the Gentiles. (Acts Chapter 10) The Lord was communicating with him by dream but Peter then had to interpret the dream himself. More often than not, that's how God inspires. Not by actual words spoken out loud but by mental and emotional sensations that point in a certain direction. When Moses meditated over how to direct his followers as they entered the Promised Land, his life experience had an influence on his prayer. His experience in Egypt as a Prince, his experience with Pharoah later, his experience with the nations around him all were no doubt taken into account when formulating a procedure for handling casualties of war. Moses set the precedent and the Jews followed the same course for many years thereafter. The reason I make such a big thing out of this, how God usually speaks to his servants, is more of a semantic issue. It is one thing to intimate that God was telling Moses in no uncertain terms, "You must kill, you must murder…" It is in an entirely different spirit for God to say, "Your inclination here is a reasonable course under the circumstances, just be judicious and fair." That is the spirit in which this injunction should be taken, I believe. Such a view is realistic and the way God handles many dubious situations when there is no perfect solution under a particular set of circumstances. Much of life's problem solving is of this caliber. We do the best we can under the circumstances!

Moses could say God told him what to do when in reality the Lord was allowing Moses to act according to what he was mulling over in his thinking process. There is a big difference between someone allowing another to perform an act when that someone is merely a by-stander and one actively goading on another toward a particular action. Our modern courts often look to distinguish culpability when a friend accompanies an associate while shopping and the associate steals an article and gets caught. The by-stander is not held liable just because his associate makes an unethical choice. When Moses set the course, God allowed Moses' people to do what they thought best since no solution was a perfect fit for their extreme circumstances. Often in the past, in the course of my business, I would be called upon by an entrepreneur who sought my advice on setting up his business start-up. The first thing I'd ask of the would-be business owner was, "What ideas do you have?" He would give me his thoughts and if they made sense I might say, "That sounds good, but remember to do such and such." No doubt my protégé might mention to another, "Paul told me this is what I should do." When in reality I simply did not discourage him when his ideas were the best under the circumstances. I did not take any credit for the entrepreneur's plans, I simply allowed him to act. So, it was with the Lord and his advice to Moses, it would appear.

And this is exactly the assessment Jesus gave of the Lord's dealings with the Jews. God allowed them to act even if what they proposed was morally wrong when it was not in God's timetable to insist on his more perfect way. Jesus gives a parallel situation that displays the Lord's reasoning that perfectly explains how God dealt with the Israelites. Look with me at Matthew 19:3-9. Picking up Jesus' conversation with some Pharisees about the propriety of divorce and loopholes Moses permitted, note Jesus' reply, "Moses permitted you to divorce your wives because your hearts were hard. But it was not this way from the beginning." (Matthew 19:8) This was another incident similar to one we discussed earlier. Do you get the point? Jesus made it clear God allowed Moses to use his discretion in adjudicating the "Law" intended from the beginning but knowing his people were not yet ready to accept the pure standard originally set. However, recall that Moses' command was still a far step above the standards of the heathen nations surrounding Moses' people. To the heathen, wives were considered property and were treated despicably. The Jews, though, had many subordinating laws to hold marriage sacred and protect wives.

Jesus helps us to see in this encounter how God operates. He is a compassionate Father who allows his people to attenuate his highest standards for a period till his time was appropriate. In this case, when the Messiah arrived on the scene, it was the befitting time to reinstate the Pure Standard of Marriage. The Lord's actions are no different for any person not yet familiar with God's standards. He does not hold their ignorance against them. He also does not hold humans' sinful weaknesses forever against them. By the same token, the Almighty took into account the Israelites just coming out from the world at that time to slowly mold them to a new, higher set of standards. Realize these two important actions God took. First, He set a higher standard of conduct within the camps of his people than the conduct expected when they were forced to deal with those outside their rule. When trading for goods among those outside people they were forced to follow the accepted rules for business transactions in the world of commerce. Similarly, when it came to warfare, they were forced to follow the rules of conduct dictated by the cruel world outside their control. The outsiders had no civil protocol for preserving the lives of women and children; they either took them as slaves or put them to death to avoid the liability. Furthermore, when non-Israelites picked a fight with the Jews there were clear expectations. The Jews knew, if they lost a battle, what the possible consequences might be, no surprises. And recall, God commanded his followers by Moses and other prophets to seek peace first before resorting to war.

Let me highlight the points being stressed here. In Jesus' comments on how Moses handled divorce, Jesus was discussing the identical time period when Moses' decisions on warfare were formulated. Jesus' comments on divorce must also apply to Moses' more serious handling of war casualties. Note, too, that Jesus mentions Moses as the final arbiter of the divorce settlement, not God. During exactly the same time period Moses issued decrees on divorce he also issued decrees on warfare. Would not Jesus' privileged understanding of the background behind the divorce decision also apply to Moses' decision on war casualties? Jesus was clear, Moses was making the final decisions based on his own wisdom and experience and they were allowed by the Lord! I'm not implying this is the only explanation that preserves unity of scripture. There may be other plausible interpretations but this one is both logical and fits with the known facts.

My suggestions appear to be the likely answer to our dilemma. One thing is sure, those who use this apparent dilemma as an excuse for not believing in God are no different than Jesus' adversaries. The lawyers and religious leaders of Jesus' time were using the identical tactics to find excuses for not wanting to believe Jesus was the promised Messiah. Each time Jesus refuted them when they attempted to put Jesus on the defensive, they would invent another excuse. Their actions belied their motives were not pure and were without any intent to acquire wisdom. Their ploy was merely a barrage of excuses. Similarly, thinkers today resort to similar ploys. They have no desire to explore Christianity for themselves. They make excuses to avoid further discussion. But they are fooling no one but themselves. Nevertheless, true believers owe it to non-believers to give them the benefit of the doubt. There are still some who truly want an answer to reasonable questions so we the believers must supply reasonable responses.

Before I rest my case, permit me to give some considerations outside the Bible to settle any loose ends. Many of you know I am a trained sociologist and here is a thought that was drummed into my head by study and experience. It is irrational to judge the past by present standards. What I mean is this. A good example can be found in the medical fields. Some of the practices of the past would be considered "barbaric" by todays values. As late as a little over one hundred years ago the practice of "bloodletting" was a standard practice. Today we can call that "barbaric." Yet, those previous generations considered themselves advanced and not barbaric. When we apply our values and what we have learned over the past centuries we must admit we are living in a very different world. To judge the past societies who had less knowledge and more superstitions by our standards is a disservice to them. This principle proves even more true when we examine habits and conventions of the past. They may be considered foolish today. By the same reasoning when it comes to warfare our present perception of the brutality of battle based on the countless historical accounts of past wars should force us to view war differently from how past generations would. During the day of our US founding fathers, the way to settle arguments was to engage in gun or sword duels. The victor was considered to have proved his position to be the most moral. One would rather risk dying in a duel than be berated as a coward. Honor was more important than life itself. Several thousand years ago, the classical Greek society judged honor to be the highest of virtues. Many a warrior, we are told, would prefer to die in battle than live a mundane, uneventful life as a farmer. During bible times most every farmer was also a fighter who lived with the threat of marauding bands of warriors surprising a peaceful village and this was an everyday way of life. What I am intimating is our experiences with and views of suffering, especially in warfare, is entirely different than those of past worlds. Don't judge the past by the present.

Similarly, we know, due to disease and limited medical knowledge whole societies have been decimated. People lived with that threat. They expected such tragedy. Every family expected there would be a good possibility one of their children would die in childbirth or within the first year of life. It was not an unusual nightmare for a mother to die in childbirth. Death was an expected fear especially among the young, let alone the old. Life expectancy in many communities was maybe forty or fifty years. When we hear of ethnic groups being exterminated in far off countries we are horrified. That is not a normal occurrence to us. Yet, in third world countries that still occurs. No, not that there is any excuse for such horror but it is treated almost as if normal when we, in a different world, would view it when happening to us as unthinkable tragedies. Again, what I am saying is when one views as "normal" the death of at least one of their children being killed by disease, one is almost forced to anticipate the worst. In an advanced society, hearing of indiscriminant child killing emits a different reaction than to those ancients. No excuse of course, but we can better understand the past by looking at things the way they did.

My reasoning, simply from a sociological perspective in addition to a biblical position, forces us to recognize the Israelites were fighting for their survival. A person on the outside judging the morality of Moses' twelve tribes might very readily conclude when that society was forced to fight, their tactics were not so unethical after all. Given that life back then was much more tenuous and that survival, even without the threat of war, was far from a sure prospect, their harsh treatment of others could be understood though not applauded. No doubt the victors could make a case for the killing of women and children after a battle was almost a kindness. After your village had been pillaged and destroyed, and then to be expected to live in the desolate aftermath, would bring additional, unbearable suffering. Conquerors reasoned that if all men in battle on the losing side were killed, what type of prospects for survival would those women and children have? Sudden death would be more compassionate than allowing them to die of starvation and the agony of months of suffering with the same end results, they reasoned. There were few other choices. They could not allow the conquered to keep living since for generations in the future the defeated would be plotting for retaliation, maybe not then, but certainly in future generations. Further, wars would be circumvented by decisive action now. That was the logical option of many pagan powers then and perhaps the logical choice of the Jews, too. What I am attempted to do is use their logic to demonstrate that even from a purely secular position, these conquering tribes might feel justified that the killing of survivors is the lesser of cruel practices.

Remember one of the reasons Jesus came was to clearly teach the Lord's fuller picture of his standards. The OT introduces us to God. It helps us to know what to expect of God and what he expects of us. It took Jesus' actual presence to answer further questions about the Lord and our individual relationships with him. The OT gave laws for a nation. Jesus addressed his instructions to individuals not to a nation (the nation of Israel). The events of the OT, though not very complimentary to the early seekers of God, demonstrate how they had to learn from experience. The cruelty and major errors of the Jews' experiences and the habits they learned from the pagan world (like killing of women and children) were a stark contrast to the beauty of a kind, loving Father whom Jesus opened our eyes to see. A case can be made for why God wanted this uncomplimentary side of early followers to be referenced as a clear delineation between how over time a loving father guides those searching for security to come to a broader picture of Him.

When Christ came, he clarified the OT laws and made them so much simpler to understand and follow. In fact, Jesus unequivocally proclaimed, "I give you a New Commandment" (John 13:34-5). New in the sense it was superior and was to be extended further in scope; new in the sense it was so concise and clear. The OT had always proclaimed that God and Love are inextricably linked. Hundreds of times God's love is mentioned. Jesus, however, revealed that God intended that we go so far as to "Love our enemies." (Matthew 5:43-8) He showed emphatically that God's love would never allow His people to engage in immoral and unethical habits of non-believers that might encroach on daily life. To love your enemies explicitly means killing of innocent mothers and children during warfare was never authorized by our father. He permitted that in the past, as Jesus showed in previous verses we have read and that has special meaning for us since he was a messenger intimate with God the Father. His words in Matthew chapter five proclaim previous leniency, there he mentioned a number of examples in this chapter were no longer going to be tolerated. Just as a parent will be much more lenient with toddlers, there comes a time when those immature, little ones had better live by the social and ethical rules of society. So the Lord as a spiritual Father allowed spiritual babes to learn by experience the consequences of following the pagan way. Jesus revealed that they, the Jews, were living by an outdated set of laws. Specifically, they were still using the rule "Love your neighbor and hate your enemy," (Matthew 5:43-8) That is not what God had in mind. Since the regiment of love took on a broader capacity, Jesus classified it a "New Command."

When reading the Hebrew Bible, the reader confronts the word "love" often. In fact, it is one of the most mentioned concepts in scripture even before the coming of Christ. Inherently the idea of love comes naturally to us without the need for extensive training. A normal child brought up with the basic needs of any human will love her parents and especially her mother. And few mothers have to be taught to love their children. In most cases they inherently have a special affection for their own. The Bible speaks of God creating mankind in his image and one of God's glaring qualities is his abundant love shown for all nature, both animate and inanimate. Scripture is replete with real life examples of historical characters who loved exceedingly and some that never could display naturally this most desirable of feelings.

Remember, the Ten Commandments start out with the concept of love. Humans were directed to "Love God" in the third commandment (Exodus 20:4). The interesting thing is when Jesus came as a representative of the Almighty, the apostle Paul described the event as, "When the Law of God approached." (Titus 3:4) With Jesus' presence among humans it was like he himself was the "Law of God." His life was the perfect epitome of how the heavenly father would live in an imperfect world and how to navigate a path that could so easily lead to danger and dead ends. What do you do when you see someone in need? Jesus showed us. What do you do when you are hated and despised? Jesus showed us. How do you react when you see suffering around us? Jesus showed us the way. He was indeed the Law of God. Observing his example was a visual picture of the "Law of God." He made it so simple to follow. Under everyday living conditions this one phrase, "Love your neighbor as yourself," fits most situations that arise, so simple so clear. And when difficult situations arose, Jesus again showed us the way. He also promised to give us the strength to accept suffering rather than retaliate with further violence.

Jesus could act in no other way. Since the Father in heaven is Love, Jesus, when here, would act no differently. As scripture reminds us, God displayed love by first conceiving the idea of sending himself, His son, the exact representation of himself. While taking on the pain of watching his son endure such suffering, He set the perfect example of unselfish love. This act shows the character of our Lord and what He values. He is love, the caring and comfort for all.

Why it seemingly took so long for him to make it clear, crystal clear, how he wanted His people to live is a question in itself. God knew humans would require generations of human experience for them to appreciate their need for God's way and His way was the best possible. He gave mankind generations to try their own way. It was thousands of years before He saw fit to start working with a whole nation of people. It took many years as a nation for the Israelites to prove to themselves and to outside observers that humans without the Lord's help were not capable of managing their own affairs successfully. The Lord allowed four hundred years and a sample size of some millions of people to prove that when they were relatively close to Him, things went well for the nation. But when they strayed, they had major problems both within their community and from other ethnic groups they came in contact with. By the time Jesus appears there had been ample time for the hundreds of cultures and thousands of societies to try on their own to perfect a government and a society that could conceive and implement a plan that really worked. But that is the way God works. He is patient and he allows for time to pass. He allows humans to put into operation not only unethical but even immoral governments who have toiled to no avail to make things right. That is just the way he works.

The only way to reconcile the Israelite treatment of other nations is to realize even pure Christianity has had to make adjustments due to a changing world. The principles are the same. A clearer picture of living God's way takes generations to perfect. The Israelites used the rubric of "an eye for an eye." And where did it come from? It was first put in written form in the Code of Hammurabi, an aspect of the law in the area from whence Abraham came. We have written documents from four hundred years before Abraham's time, that is two thousand years before Jesus came, proclaiming those exact words. Imagine, for millennia that was the law of the land in the Middle East.

To this day the nation of modern Israel lives by this principle. That is one of the reasons there will never be peace in that continent. Even Islam, which traces their origin to the same Abraham of the Jews, lives by this same code. In our own day, when Jews are bombing, or when Moslems are bombed, the rule is exactly the same, you bomb, and we bomb back, and both ethnic groups repeat the exact same words, "Eye for an Eye." They espouse a completely different set of values than those of Jesus. They call this justice but in reality, all it does is perpetuate injustice Our world has never found the perfect balance of employing both cold objective logic and creative subjective intuition and inspiration to display wisdom. We must approach scripture applying those same tools. The objective events portrayed in scripture and the subjective seemingly mythological aspects are both needed as a combination for expansive living. My faith, personally, is based, not on the biblical stories of old, but on observing every-day living and noticing how applying biblical standards invariably bring the most successful and gratifying results. Jesus' clarification of original Hebrew standards really works in contrast to the standards of the previous four thousand years before him as actual written history attests and I observe daily.

The idea of justice is a main tenet of all societies and that is no doubt why the "Eye for an Eye" theme has been popular for thousands of years. Since at least 1900 B.C., that is four thousand years, societies repeat the same words without realizing what they are espousing. The problem is this mentality assures that someone innocent always seems to get hurt, especially women and children. The person who originally and publicly disavowed this mentality was Jesus. Jesus implied follow this rule is the easy way out but it only perpetuates the problem and alienates people. A current example in society is our attempt to resolve past racial issues with affirmative action, definitely a laudable goal. But without thinking it through others are hurt. Lately in the news, we hear Asian students say they are being discriminated against since many cannot get into top colleges like Harvard when other less qualified minorities are welcomed to fill quotas. How much better to resolve discrimination with inventive ideas that do not hurt other groups inadvertently. That is a study and the topic of discussion in itself in our quest for justice we hope will be pondered. Jesus' position on injustice is one of the reasons I personally am a Christian; his goal is always to resolve injustice without hurting or discriminating against anyone at the same time. And one of the goals of my paper has been to put the blame for continuing injustice where it belongs, not on God, but on the people and rules they make that fall short of rectifying and can exaggerate problems.

I would like to finish this treatise by summarizing what I have come to understand about these difficult sets of ancient practices of early believers in the God of the Bible. I see no conflict with Christian ethics. I have given possible explanations that appear, in my thinking, to fully explain any apparent discrepancies between then and now. What I have attempted to show is that there need not be a conflict between belief in a God of Love and the cruel treatment he tolerated by his people. This issue is no different than the question of why a loving God would tolerate evil in the world, a topic I have discussed in great detail in another of my treatises elsewhere. I have attempted to analyze the glaring example of inhumane behavior by the Israelites, purportedly God's people, from multiple angles and I'm satisfied that an apparent contradiction in standards which might give reason to discredit Christianity is a fallacy.

First of all, Christian doctrine never, ever has condoned the unethical history of their forebears, the early Jews. I must highlight that even Jesus took up the issue and refuted the behavior of his ancestors stating emphatically that mankind had not been ready for the ultimate mandates of pure Christianity. And I have suggested we may need to rethink how we interpret scripture which on the surface seems to suggest God, through his actual words, encouraged warriors on to immoral treatment of the conquered. In this one isolated period of some four hundred years as a sovereign nation, those God-chosen men acted out of character from His standards. However, there is a vast difference when comparing when Moses testified and gave actual proof that God dictated to him the Ten Commandments, which were actually written, and his claim or feeling that God was telling him to follow the standards of warfare extant at the time. Was he simply following the standard practice of the times as we have suggested?

I am appealing to each of you readers to judge for yourselves to what extent the God of Christianity and Jesus are to be connected to the behavior of the pre-Messiah tribes of a thousand years prior to Jesus. I advise that Christians be aware of the facts and background of ancient Israel so that they can defend the message of the Way of Jesus. This way, when someone who is a sincere seeker of truth questions the Old Testament accounts of inhumane practice, they can have multiple answers at hand to defend the reputation of Jesus and the God of the Bible. And just as important, continue inventing new measures to fight injustice in the world.

Chapter 9

Rich In Every Way

If we are ever to feel like independent fully functioning adults in this world, each of us must come to what I call a "balanced view of money, wealth and riches." Our society, unfortunately, does not seem to want to allow us this option. The media entices us to seek wealth to find happiness on one extreme. On the other extreme, if we happen to be born into poverty, both our fellow peers and many in the government would just as soon push us to try to get by with government assistance. Further, some Christians feel one cannot be a true believer without taking what amounts to a vow of poverty. When it comes to decision making, I have found there is something to be said for what the philosopher of old, Aristotle, called the "Golden Mean" or the proper decision balance in cases like this. That is the purpose of this paper. I propose a "Balanced View" of Money, Assets, Wealth. I simply suggest our goal with money is to ultimately be able to live so that money is no longer a major issue in one's life. What that means and how to get there is my assignment here. Whether one chooses to have more than enough or just desires to get by, either way, a balanced perspective permits one to feel fulfilled and satisfied.

When we hear talk about money, we're talking hundreds of possible options. I am going to use the Christian view as a model for what I have come to find is a well- balanced view. Historically some of the wealthiest believers in the Bible were among the richest of men who ever lived but, at the same time, some of the greatest heroes of the past were those who took that vow of poverty. My thesis is that both of those extremes can be that perfect balance! And while there are other possible positions from other religions, other philosophies and other financial perspectives possible, and some may actually be as astute as the Christian view, the Christian model is one that I know to work from all angles and in the end brings true satisfaction. I know, because I have studied it thoroughly, done research studies as an academic and lived by it successfully for many years. However, when we talk about Christian advice on money, you'll get hundreds of different views. Inquire of a Christian who's taken what amounts to a vow of poverty, you get one opinion; inquire of a Christian who's given thousands of dollars per year to charities and you get another perspective. Totally different perhaps. My perspective here may well be quite different yet. I am writing as a Christian of over fifty years, a Christian theologian for over forty years, a financial planner for over thirty years and a Charitable Benefactor for over twenty years. This paper takes in all those perspectives. I think I can offer a viewpoint from a qualified expert you probably won't get elsewhere and a model which brings both a successful attitude toward and management of money. The important point is we'll discuss how to be RICH in the ways that count.

You've no doubt heard that Jesus' discourses recorded in the Bible talk more about money and material possessions than practically any other topic. And there's a reason for this. Jesus taught what has come to be called "Practical Christianity." And what is more practical than understanding how to provide financially for our everyday existence? Where will we get the funds for today's food and material trappings? Jesus taught about frugality, counting the cost of major purchases, making money work for you, on and on. With all that advice and living in an industrial society, the Americas, Europe and much of the Far East, a Christian normally should have very little difficulty providing for his needs. I'm talking about a practicing Christian here. But I want to go a step further and discuss prudence toward money, the proper attitude toward money and a concept like what has come to be called "Prosperity Gospel."

First let's clear the air. Money and a discussion about money is not an evil. Jesus talked about taking care of and seeing that our money works for us. Remember the Wicked Servant in Jesus' parable was chastised for not putting money in the bank to draw interest? (Matthew 25:24-27) Remember, too, early Christians in the First and Second Century congregated in the homes of the more well to do believers who had homes. One such person mentioned by name in scripture is Lydia (Acts 16:14) who was purportedly a well-to-do charitable woman.

It is no different today. Theoretically most Christians in developed countries, following Jesus' advise and the advice in The Proverbs, Ecclesiastes and the Psalms in the Bible, should have no difficulty making ends meet. That is, unless they have come from addiction, mental disability, being in an abusive relationship or never having been given guidance in money management. In any case, being part of a church community can help in these situations. A good many believers who have worked regularly and faithfully for a corporation have pensions or retirement savings today. As a result, they are able to not only not be a burden to others but can contribute to the needs of those not quite so fortunate. Further, in most developed countries, any person who contributes to Social Security and contributes to her company's pension plan could have much more than enough for her retirement plan, as long as she is prudent. Hopefully many of you should feel rich financially already. Before we go on, one caveat. If we so desire, most citizens in a developed country can be rich but there is no guarantee those riches will endure. Any number of eventualities can destroy wealth overnight. However, please don't be so foolish to say, "Since money today cannot be guaranteed, why even bother trying to accumulate it." Even Jesus warned about such a narrow view. If you are counting on your kids taking care of you in old age, or you have no concern about forgoing a lifesaving operation for a family member because you cannot afford the deductible, that is your choice. But don't discourage a friend or especially a fellow Christian from following Jesus' prudent advice about saving for the unknown. Please, let them make their own choices.

Unfortunately, many Christians only concern themselves with Jesus' spiritual guidance. There are those who have just come back to or just found out about Christianity who may have major financial problems to start with. From my financial counseling work of over thirty years, I must say, this should never be the case unless there are extreme circumstances. A good many Christians who worked regularly and faithfully for a corporation now live on pensions today. They tell me all the time, "When I was a young immature Christian, I thought it foolish to put money away for a pension I'd probably never be able to use, but I'm so glad now that I did not follow that childish thinking. And as a result, they do not need to be a burden on others but can contribute toward the needs of those not so fortunate with income. The problem is for the newly converted Christian who did not have the benefit of biblical advice on finance in his or her younger formative income years. We can only hope a nearby church will help those so afflicted.

This leads us to the issue I find debated in Christian circles. We ask, does the Gospel, a term for the Good News from the Bible, include any promise of prosperity for us now, in this life, regardless of what we believe about a possible life to come? In other words, will living by the tenets set forth by Jesus and scripture give us any financial benefit in our present life? Some Christians flatly say, "No, my reward will come in the life to come. I'll get my reward when I go to heaven." While another Christian says, "Yes, I see throughout scripture the promise is often made that living by the practice standards from the Bible leads to a measure of prosperity and abundance now." Very often I've found that seeming contradictions in interpretation can be easily settled by first going back to the terms being used in communication. Just the other day I was talking to someone about our county commissioner and I remarked how reasonable and efficient she was. The person I was talking to vehemently protested, "She's the most irresponsible manager I've ever had to deal it!" We soon realized we were talking about two different people. And that's often the case with any seeming biblical conflict as, for example, financial benefits offered to spiritual seekers in this life where the problem may simply be the type of financial rewards we're speaking of.

To first set the record straight, I admit I came to my own personal conclusion on my attitude toward money when I first became a Christian. And that was long before, actually twenty-five years before, I heard terms like "Prosperity Gospel." Therefore, I don't feel I have to potentially disqualify myself from giving my unbiased comments. But I'll let you be the judge. You see, I became a Christian when I was a teenager. As part of my making a decision on which road or path I'd choose to go down in life, I happened upon the words of Jesus in Matthew chapter 6. Here Jesus expounded on not being anxious about material possessions, like food, clothing and in that context, he mentioned the lilies of the field and remarked, "Not even Solomon in all his glory was arrayed as one of these (lily flowers)." Being a self-conscious, introverted young kid who lacked confidence, I latched on to the words, "Do not be anxious." Then I read verse 33 (Matthew 6:33), "Seek first the kingdom and His righteousness and these other things will be added to you." Not knowing any better, I believed what Jesus said literally and there and then agreed to the proposition he made me. I'll seek the Kingdom, since I felt inside it's the right thing to do, and all I wanted was to know I'm being taken care of and be guided along. Subconsciously I thought of that part about having the self-confidence of King Solomon which was an added bonus to me as a self-conscious teen.

So here I am, over fifty years later. After these many years of trying to "seek first the Kingdom" with varying degrees of success, I look back and it all came true, every dream and everything I took Jesus' words to mean have come true. Everything I could ever need has been provided. In fact, though I never dreamed so, even all the material things I could ever have needed has been "added" to me as Jesus said. I've gotten far, far more than I could ever have dreamed of asking for. I hadn't asked for much when I first took Jesus up on his proposition. This was before having enough money meant any-thing to me for I, at least, was brought up in a lower working-class home but we always had enough to eat. Back then, too, I never had reason to comprehend such a thing as "unrequited love," since I had parents I knew really cared about me though they made their own share of mistakes in raising me. All I wanted was to find confidence and becoming a competent adult but I ended up with a whole lot more! So, from my own experience I have to say there is something to be said about this idea of "Christian prosperity," which I felt I had though our family didn't have a great deal of money.

So far, I have been emphasizing having the proper attitude toward money, wealth and finances. One of the points I strive to stress is that of being a good steward of the assets entrusted to each of us. I have been intimating that having "enough" is not difficult to attain if one follows the biblical principles regarding financial assets. Though this piece is not the venue for discussing those principles in detail, I will mention several ideas to prove my contention. As I mentioned at the beginning, comprehending one or two simple ideas can all but guarantee that money will not be a major issue in one's life. And that is assuming a worker is willing to take a job when one is available. I learned that from my dad. He never finished high school but he always had a job. We, as a family, always had a meal on the table. Though his trade was as a carpenter and at times the construction industry was slow and people weren't building as readily, such as in recessions, yet he always found some kind of work.

So, given that a worker is willing to take any kind of job temporarily, even one "beneath" him or her, these two simple rules I present now will ensure that any individual would not unlikely to have serious financial issues. The first rubric is the simple one to avoid charging purchases on a credit card with no intention of paying all those debts in full each month. It isn't long before those small purchases, let alone larger ones, if left to accumulate over several months, can become an insurmountable burden too difficult to make minimum payments on. A normal family should rarely have installment payments other than for a house and perhaps a car. Making it a practice to pay off credit card balances each month should be simple enough for anyone to understand and comply with. The difficulty may be living by such a practice over the long term. This is where cultivating the virtue of patience is required, patience to wait to save up for an item first before buying. That's how you avoid getting into an uncontrollable debt situation in the first place. This is a simple enough biblical rule to comprehend but it may take a firm resolve to live by.

The other financial tip I have is proactive and again not difficult to live yet it will actually help a prudent person start to "feel rich" is this. When I relate it to you as the reader, you may immediately brush it off as being too simple and too impossible to be true. It isn't and I only wish you'd try it before passing judgement. I am writing here from my own experience and that of many eager students I've counseled. I have always been a very conservative spender which comes from living with parents who both lived a childhood and young adulthood trying to survive during the worst financial deprecation the world, not just the United States, has ever known. They were forced, out of necessity, to learn the art of economizing if they were to survive. I inherited that mindset. As a result, I rarely had financial emergencies myself even as a young adult with family. We always got by. However, it took me till I was close to age fifty when I began to wonder, "Why is it that though we, as a household, have enough monetarily don't I feel contented?" I've always found, as I did then, that whenever I thought and prayed regularly about a matter, eventually I find an answer. In this case, whether it was a person I talked to or a book I read, in either case I was led to discover my problem was not money but an improper attitude and nothing more. To prove it to myself, I asked, "When is it that I feel inadequate with regard to money?" The answer was clear. I retorted, "Truthfully the only time is when an emergency arises and I need to buy a new refrigerator, a new stove, a major purchase when we have not planned for it." And this was the suggestion I learned: I needed to take a few months to accumulate an "emergency fund," whatever amount I personally required to feel assured I'd have funds ready for my next emergency. I think, at the time, I decided five thousand dollars would be sufficient. This amount did not take too long to collect, a little from a surplus in my checking account, a couple months of putting off a discretionary purchase, whatever. Once I had those funds secured in a separate bank savings account that I promised I'd only touch in an emergency did I realize, "I really do have enough money." Within six months, sure enough, I needed some of those funds for whatever, a major repair of some sort, I can't remember, but I had the money ready. This cemented my new habit. I then took another few months to regroup and collect funds equal to what I spent on the last emergency. Not long after that I built up my fund more ambitiously. It was like magic! I began to feel free of the burden of thinking I'm always having to play "catch up." I exclaimed, "I absolutely feel rich! I have no reason to feel like I'm having to live as if I was perpetually in financial danger." Sure enough, what changed for me was attitude. Many of you, my readers, may already have more than enough in your checking account but by making the distinction of segregating your emergency money to a separate account you are psychologically affirming to yourself you do have adequate funds. You'll find, as I did, you will be able to exclaim, "You know, I am rich too."

I (we) can say that with one proviso, though. I always remind myself when it comes to material assets, one can never have full security in this world and in this life. Some of the richest people in history have lost everything no matter how hard they tried to keep it. To this day, I remind myself regularly. "I'm blessed with an abundance and can live accordingly as long as I do not lull myself into feeling I have absolute security. The is no such thing!" So why be frantic about attaining something that does not even exist? Be content having more than enough. That's what I'd like all my readers to sense. There is so much more I can tell you about material wealth but those two simple lessons are among the most crucial and will provide any reader with a good starting point to manage finances.

Saying that, let's talk about the one verse that makes the proper view of money and material things so clear. This was written by a writer who testified how his own life was transformed, a transformation far more startling than mine. He was Paul, the apostle of Jesus, and he clarified financial issues for me when, in the course of time, I came upon this verse anew. He wrote in 2 Corinthians 9:10-11, "He who supplies seed to the sower, bread for food, will also supply and increase your share of seed and will enlarge the harvest of your righteousness. You will be made rich in every way so that you can be generous on every occasion, and through your generosity will result in thanksgiving to God." I believe if you can understand every part of this verse, you'll know pretty much everything you need to know about money and material success in this life! Please read this over carefully, preferably directly from any Bible yourself. Take the time to go over every word. Paul uses the illustration of seed for food and bread for sustenance but the most important point to him is having the harvest of one's righteousness enlarged. Yes, physical food, material things are necessities of life and God promises to provide them but non-material "Righteousness" is what he zeros in on. When one is assessed as being "righteous" he or she has what is really needed and wanted. So, when we read about God promising to give you the abundance of our heart's desire, scripture makes it clear there is a difference between what we need and what we think we need, that is, what we want.

I see this all the time with my grandchildren. They want, they think they need, the latest Star Wars characters and paraphernalia, but shortly after opening the gifts they end up playing with the boxes the toys came in. They thought they needed something, material toys, but what they really wanted was just something to play with. And what they "needed" and didn't realize, was being given attention and the feeling that goes with knowing someone really cares about them as individuals. Wants and needs, again, what I learned from Paul here and what I learned from my own experience as reaffirmed in practical living. Take Jesus' words and hundreds of Bible verses at face value when they assert, you'll be given an abundance and you'll be prosperous as seekers of the Kingdom, those promises are real. You are promised, not what you think you want, but what you actually need. When I got what I really needed, though, at the time, I didn't even know what it was. I bargained for self-confidence, what a teenager desperately needs or at least thinks he needs. But I got an "abundance" more than self-confidence, including unconditional love, life satisfaction, fulfillment, peace of mind. And I keep getting more of these as time goes on.

Let me give you an example from my own life. Probably the one thing I wanted most in life, something I wanted and didn't have, was a well-rounded education. I say that because what I really needed, I already had, being a Christian in the company of other Christians. I was engaged to be married by the time I was twenty-one, having stumbled upon a life partner who was to teach me what unconditional love really is, over the years, I never consciously dreamed of those true needs on my own. However, a fulfilling academic education is something I didn't have. Shortly after getting married, my wife became pregnant so I was forced to work to provide and my education became a fleeting dream. I put it out of mind till I was thirty. Only then did that burning desire return again. If I could only get an Associate of Arts college degree, I'd be perfectly happy. And in short order I did get that degree. I celebrated that accomplishment for all of one day till I realized I had to have a Bachelor of Arts degree. So, I began working toward that goal. No sooner did I get that designation I again reveled in that accomplishment for a day or two and realized I hadn't fulfilled my desire. The same happened when I received my Master of Business Administration. I then actually commenced my PhD studies, as before, the satisfaction and the exhilaration of attaining that goal lasted a few weeks. I say this because what I thought I wanted, education, was not what I really needed inside. What I really needed was the feeling I had enough life experience of the proper kind and the assistance from a Higher Source that I could confidently face whatever adversity I confronted and have the courage to look it in the eye, face to face without backing down. What I thought I needed was academic education but what I really needed was life experience enhanced by the writings of authors I never studied while in universities. Fortunately, I have gotten what I needed since then but that's a story for another time. What I've been saying is what I thought I "wanted" is not what I "needed." Only when I had what I wanted did I realize that was not what I really needed. So back to scripture. God promised abundance and prosperity to all who "seek first the Kingdom." I keep stressing "needs" and "wants." There is a big difference. Normally, with "wants" you never have enough, you'll always desire more. But needs are satisfying, fulfilling, sustaining.

So, there's the first part of 2 Corinthians 4. But the curious thing is what Paul claims in verse eleven. Notice, the Apostle says, "You will be made rich in every way." So, from his experience, he's averring the

Lord will "in every way" provide "riches" as needed to any follower of Christ. In other words, the gifts from the Lord can include material riches, that's part of "every way." Permit me to put in my two cents here. Talking to many other Christians who are well off materially, they invariably give thanks to God for their abundance materially and acknowledge that through Jesus' guidance and blessings they have that material abundance. I can also testify from my own experience. It has been due to my own efforts, attempting to live by Bible principles learned from scripture like living prudently, saving for the future and not living extravagantly, that I personally am not in need financially. I have followed Jesus' advice on handling money, along with the practical wisdom from the Bible books of Ecclesiastes, Proverbs and the Psalms. I've, therefore, been able to avoid undue risk with funds by not willfully attempting to amass wealth as a primary concern. I've invested wisely as Jesus counseled in the parable of the talents. I truly have been blessed and I give thanks to the Lord for his advice from a practical standpoint. I could not have done it on my own. He gave me the tools, I only had to put forth the effort.

Then finally, let's not forget the final part of the Apostle's remarks on riches. Again, in verse 12 (2 Corinthians 9:11, 12) he reminds us of what is the measure and value of riches. "So that you be generous on every occasion, and through us your generosity will result in thanksgiving to God." This is the ultimate. A Christian can expect to be provided riches in every way so that they can be generous on "every occasion." Ultimately the proper use of any type of wealth will bring thanksgiving to God. Isn't scripture so clear here? Being "rich in every way" means whatever wealth or whatever things of value at our disposal, whether those riches be time, talents, material treasures, blessings, wellbeing, are to be available to others in their time of need. I personally would wish that any fortune I may have left when

I pass on will be given to charities and ministries to be used wisely so that those who receive them can give "thanksgiving" to God. To me, scripture is saying that by living confidently and knowing the Lord will provide, there will always be riches there to share with others. There is no end to the riches God can provide for our needs.

To be sure we understand the point made, the Apostle states the profound message in yet another way in a preceding verse (2 Corinthians 9:8). "And God is able to make all grace abound to you, that IN ALL THINGS, AT ALL TIMES, having all you need, you will abound in every good work." How reassuring to know God promises followers "all you need." Again, "all grace abounds" to us so that we are able to do "good works." And not just sparingly, for whatever we have has been given to us providentially, whatever we are blessed with, be it time, talents, treasures and trust, we are to use what we've been given to do good works.

So far, we conclude that Jesus does provide all our needs and we've established those needed can include all types of prosperity. But lest we should come to Christianity with the goal of having abundance only, Jesus cautions us that there is a price to pay. It's not all "fun and games" so to speak. There is a sobering proviso that comes with all the blessings accruing to a believer now in this life. Jesus gives us the full picture, the reality of this life. Jesus' own words recorded at Mark 10:29-30 has the full picture. "I tell you the truth, no one who has left homes or brothers or sisters or mother or father or children or fields for me and the gospel will fail to receive a hundred times as much IN THIS PRESENT AGE (homes, brothers, sister, mothers, children- and with them persecutions) and in the age to come, eternal life." Jesus cautions us that being a follower of Jesus will bring adversity, yes, but along with a hundred-fold blessings. I am just worried that many Christians have not understood the BALANCED view and needlessly choose to live in poverty thinking that is what God wants of them.

Now to complete our understanding of how our training as Jesus' disciples might be of assistance in our present existence, we return to the words of the Apostle Paul. So often in scripture we find a short pithy verse that, in a few words, clarifies our perceptions. One of those is found at 1 Timothy 4:8. Simply stated, "For physical training is of some value, but godliness has value FOR ALL THINGS, holding promise for BOTH THE PRESENT LIFE and the life to come." Paul's assertion based on his life experience was that "godliness" and discipleship training is valuable even in our present life. What we learn from Jesus and Christian teaching can help us get on in this life. The Bible is replete with real life stories of faithful, godly men and women who profited financially directly as a result of their closeness with God. Immediately comes to mind Joseph, Esther, Daniel, the Patriarchs, on and on we can recite examples. Each would probably never gain material riches if they had not been following the tenets of Godly living. No, spiritual intelligence, in itself does not guarantee material wealth. It does, however, guarantee WEALTH. Material wealth can easily be lost through no fault of the possessor while true wealth conferred by the Lord cannot be lost without the consent of the possessor. This is the critical difference, which I hope sinks in for each of us. The stock market goes up and down, the monetary systems of every government and society can collapse but the sensations of spiritual wealth, like peace of mind and happiness can never be taken away without one's willfully and consistently allowing it to slip away!

Over the years I have observed incredible wealth created if a person sets that status as an overarching goal, it can be attained. Those willing to work for financial wealth often attain it. Such success is irrespective of godliness. However, very often, a godly person who is willing to work hard and who puts himself in an environment conducive to wealth finds that his qualities, honed by godliness (such qualities as loyalty, patience, persistence, faith etc.) are the ingredients that allow him to excel even in the business world. This observation can easily be demonstrated by secular, sociological research, though this is not the time to expand on such studies. You don't have to be a Christian to have patience, perseverance or faith, anyone can see their practical value. However, a Christian learns to perfect those qualities simply because it is the right thing to do. He or she soon learns those are also the qualities that are of practical value in business, for instance. I would contend if a Christian wishes to pursue financial wealth as one of her pursuits, the use of these Christian virtues will be one of the means she will find most valuable in her journey. I would challenge you to talk to any of the millions of Christians who are financially well off, other than by inheritance; they will admit success came because of godly virtues even without them consciously using them.

I have to say from my own experience, it is easy to misinterpret scripture. To think only of physical possessions, "things," when you read of riches or wealth in the Bible. For example, King David, a wealthy man, makes claims from his own experience with the Lord, and gives his testimony at Psalm 34:4. He claims the Father will give us "the delights of our life." However, by reading his songs you come to find he sung most eloquently about his gifts from God that were not materially lavish. In fact, most of us when forced to meditate and choose between a brand-new house, say, well-appointed and paid for, or the guarantee of a happy long-term marriage and close relations with family, would choose the latter, the idyllic family life over the material benefits. I try to remember often what is most important to me. Over the years I personally have formulated my list of "delights of life." Close relationships with others come toward the top of the list. This comradery is not physical, it's the emotional support, sensation of being cared for, the connection to others that counts. By far the personal satisfaction of being loved and being able to love is most cherished. The satisfaction of being contented and being sheltered by others is worth more than anything material. Having a sense of fulfillment that my life has meaning and purpose is exhilarating. The sheer joy of BEING ALIVE cannot be compared to any personal possessions. Any believer, using wisdom through meditation, learns that material possessions can only provide more options, more choice, but never more long-term satisfaction.

Coming back now to our original question, what about the idea of Christian principles leading to a sense of prosperity? We must admit, yes, scripture often talks in literally hundreds of places, Old and New Testament, of material riches being offered to the godly. However, in most all cases, these offers are never meant to be the terminal goals of life. And never do they encourage an all-encompassing motive of gaining the material advantages. The motive as we have read is wealth for generosity's sake. Money for money's sake, money as an end in itself is an illusion. It can only bring short term pleasures. Yet money for generosity's sake can and does bring long term satisfaction. And without a doubt, living by godly principles and striving to evince godly virtues will also make it much easier for one to attain material wealth as a by-product of a godly quest. Fortunately, there are many millions of Christians that count their blessings by being able to give an extra portion from their abundance to help others and provide resources to help those less fortunate hear the message of Good News. I was recently talking to one such person. He confides that over the years, though his income for many years was no more than average, he was able to prepare modestly for retirement. And since his family tried to live frugally, was able to accumulate an abundance. He is now able to give away tens of thousands of dollars every year to church and to help those in need. He acknowledges, "Little did I imagine the good I've been able to do by just trying to be a good steward of the money coming through our household."

Yes, prosperity and gospel are compatible. However, never ever may such talk be dangled as a sole incentive for pursuing holiness. The apostle gives all the incentive necessary to seeking wealth. Abundance gives us all the opportunity to give generously, to feel the joy that comes with "more happiness in giving than receiving." And most of all as noted in 1 Corinthians, "And through your generosity will result in thanksgiving going to God." What greater feeling of worth than to know our small human efforts will result in thanksgiving being given to God. I heartily recommend this balanced view of money. The wisdom from ancient times puts it this way, "Money is a defense." So well put. What's more important as the wiseman said, "…but godliness is good for all things." Don't squander or treat with little regard the money that flows through your hands weekly. We are encouraged to "do good" with whatever we have.

Chapter 10

When The Thrill Of Living Is Gone

Is the thrill of living still there? It's a question many have probably never asked. Also, some might have a mild trepidation confronting what might be considered a threatening question. I would, though, like to see you ask this question of yourself. Now, don't dwell on it, but be honest with yourself. Even if you can't answer affirmatively when you ask yourself, "Is the thrill of living still within me?" This short article will help you feel the thrill is still there. I know there have been times in all our lives, perhaps as a teenager or as a child or an adult you remember that feeling of exhilaration, when you could say, "It's great to be alive." This will come back.

If you don't currently have that sense of excitement, wouldn't you like to have it back? I've found, for myself at least, the first step is to consciously realize the thrill of living just isn't as strong as it used to be. Ask yourself, "What happened? What's missing? Have my circumstances changed, am I missing a happy family, a loyal friendship, exciting opportunities or prospects?" I found, for myself, just a recognition that my thrill of living had been misplaced somehow and a determination to get it back, was all that was required. As a sociologist I've learned that individuals in our society frequently go through predictable periods in life when they are more prone to life disruptions, times when we are unsure of where we're going. Such age periods are between age 18 and 21, then again around age 30 and again around mid-life, say age 45 and finally retirement are all examples. Some have called these periods "Passages" when in transition from one lifestyle to another. There may be career uncertainty, family uncertainty, and times of self-evaluation. Predictably we may not be the most settled then and we may not take the time for meditation, enjoyment, recreation or exploring. That's why it's good from time to time to self-evaluate and ask, "Do I still have that thrill of living? Do I appreciate the opportunity that being alive affords me?"

I remember one such time of evaluation in my life. I was 29, married, one child, no meaningful career, never completed my education but, thankfully, I was honest with myself. I admitted I was bored and had few expectations. I realized something was wrong. I began to ask, "How had this predicament happened, I hadn't planned it?" How exactly was it that I went from being on my own for the first time, forming a long-term relationship with my wife, having a child, being an adult but all of a sudden realizing I wasn't thrilled to be alive? For me I realized I didn't have any meaningful, exciting goals or intriguing prospects ahead. I pondered and over the next few months realized what was missing. Among other things I asked myself, "What was it that was different about the times when I had the thrill of living?" I admitted I hadn't finished my education. I didn't have a meaningful career. I hadn't thought about the next pages in my future other than maybe a day or two ahead. But I was very fortunate, the one thing

I had going for me at the time was I was a Christian having tenets which insisted I be brutally honest with myself. I am not talking religious Christianity; I am talking the Christian principles that have stood the test of time for thousands of years were still with me. I realized, at my low point, Christianity is goal oriented, it teaches the concept of realistic self-esteem, living circumspectly, deriving meaning in life and the importance of service for true happiness. I just had to remember what I already knew. Similarly, most religions and even secular religions emphasize those same ideas. These are spiritual truths not just religious truths. The transition for me was relatively simple. I concluded what goals were most compelling to me and what outcomes were of prime importance.

So what can you do? To answer that, let me relate to you a fortunate meeting I had with someone not many years after finally taking the path to purposeful living. This was at my 25th high school reunion. Though many of my old friends had moved to other parts of the country, I couldn't help but anticipate reuniting with all those best friends. There was Ken whose big dream was to be accepted and graduate from West Point, and he did. There was Doug who had applied to a prestigious engineering college, and he succeeded. And then there was Eleanor who dreamed of being an activist before the term was invented; she graduated from Harvard and built on those connections. I couldn't help but wonder, though, if they were still as excited about their lives as they were when I first knew them? One thing about high school reunions, an alumnus does his best to put his life circumstances in the best light. It's almost impossible to discern a classmate's true level of success or well-being on the surface. But there was one person when you talked to him, you didn't have to guess. He was my old high school counselor. Yes, Mr. Clark, he was there. I had remembered him 25 years before, a man in his fifties but now looking all of 75 or 80. He couldn't wait to tell everyone what he was doing. "After I retired I started working at a Day Care Center in the inner city," he volunteered, "and have been working there ever since. When I can teach a 4 year old to tie her shoes and she is so proud, there is no experience in the world quite as exhilarating as that. Every day, new experiences, new challenges. I'm just happy to be alive." Right there and then I promised myself I was going to be just like Mr. Clark when I grew up. (I felt I wasn't fully grown up yet though in my 40's). I'm still counting on that promise coming true.

We all need that feeling. In fact, I'm wondering if when the thrill of living is gone we start the dying process? So how do we get it back? Let me be clear what I mean by "the thrill of living." We have all experienced being excited, feeling intuitive, expecting adventures, new experiences, opening to new sensations, having goals and plans and knowing it might be a little scary but exhilarating. How do we get back there? I think the first step is to remind ourselves how we felt when living was a thrill.

Next, here's the advice of someone, contemplating the past but really very depressed when he first began reminiscing. He's the writer of a book within the Bible called Ecclesiastes. If you're not necessarily a believer, don't worry, it has nothing to do with religion. If you found this short volume randomly written somewhere without reference to the Bible you'd think the writer was just an average old man reminiscing about life, someone going through a bout of depression actually. However, as you read more closely you see this is actually the writing of a very wise philosopher who appears to have gone through that "thrill of living is gone" phase himself. But he's wise enough to look back at the times when he was excited and happy. Listen to his thoughts.

First of all he insists much of life simply unfolds despite our plans and efforts to accomplish an optimal outcome. "The race is not to the swift…It's Time and Unforeseen Chance occurrence," that plays its part (Eccl. 9:11) You have plans, perhaps coming out of high school or college and the world beckons you with welcoming arms. But it doesn't always work out the way of your plans. Events happen and you're caught up in an environment that's not productive or stimulating. Don't be upset, most of us have had that experience at least a few times. Along the way, though, you do have happy times, productive periods. Enjoy them while you can. Unfortunately, many have never learned to enjoy the moment. Here's the Wiseman's assessment (Eccl. 5:13), "When God gives someone wealth and possessions and the ability to enjoy them, to accept his lot and be happy in his toil-that is the Gift of God." Ponder this for a moment. I've learned from experience when it says here "God gives" it's not like the author is claiming God is playing favorites. Personally, when I found the wisdom of thousands of years' experience, wisdom I felt was inspired by a higher source, "God given" if you will, I found a real treasure. I acquired wealth and possessions as the writer possessed. But much of that wealth wasn't necessarily material possessions so much as other treasures like Wisdom, Inspiration, Friends, Family. But even that's not what delivers happiness. The writer emphasizes the main ingredient, "The ability to enjoy them." Here's the point. How many people have you heard of with all those possessions but who are not really happy? What's missing is the enjoyment and appreciation. Over the years I found those having truly exciting, meaningful lives have come to the same conclusion. One recently told me, "I don't want to ever have to look back at a present moment and regret that I didn't enjoy it at the time." So everyday make time to appreciate what one has. And the advice is not just for those with abundant possessions since we all know inherently our dearest possessions are not material. All along the way, every little success, every little blessing, recognize them, appreciate them, an "Attitude of Gratitude" I call it.

The Wiseman next injects "accept your lot." What I think he's saying is, "Yes, go ahead and keep striving but enjoy any measure of success you do find along the way. Enjoy the moment, enjoy the journey." Never be so busy worrying about the past or assuming only the future can possibly bring you happiness. Unless you build that attitude of gratitude to take with you on your life journey you may never feel settled or secure. Enjoy it while you have it. And again, "There is nothing better than for a man to enjoy his work." (Eccl.3:22) Current studies by psychologists have verified that a major ingredient of life happiness is exactly as the Wiseman found, a job you enjoy. He further cautions whatever we do along the way will always come back to us. We'll be evaluated or repaid in ways we'd never begin to imagine. (Eccl. 11:9) I recommend you read the little book, Ecclesiastes, found in the Bible. Think about the lesson given by a one-time pessimistic old man who eventually puts it all in perspective.

Finally, here are a few ideas others have suggested on how they stopped feeling sorry for themselves and started living again. Mr. Clark's, my counselor's, story, I just told, is a good starting point. He found a way to put meaning back into his existence. So many possibilities. You may not even be religious but why not consider joining with a church that makes its mission helping the community? I suggest a church or private service organization since some have mentioned their experiences, similar to mine, that government sponsored groups are so stifled by bureaucracy that the potential seems never to be attained. What about volunteering at a public school to tutor little kids with their reading? Volunteer for programs that mentor single parents, assisting them to venture back into society and the workforce without addicting them to a life of welfare hand-outs. There's Habitat for Humanity and Toys for Tots at Christmas Time. There is something about the human spirit that causes it to soar when it knows it is helping another!

Hobbies too are great sources of inspiration. I know many gardeners who have "come back to life" by nurturing their flowering plants to "come back to life." One simple way to decide on a personal project is to just daydream about your interests as a young child. What were you good at, what did you enjoy doing? If you haven't continued with those interests, why not? What is it you always wanted to learn more about but never took the time to pursue further? So many things to do, so little time for all of them!

All these suggestions, if pursued will become, as the Wiseman said, "the Gift of God." There is nothing more wonderful, more valuable than enjoying your life in the moment. So valuable that it could be classified, "The Gift of God." Accepting the Wisdom of the Ages, pursuing that path, finding life is meaningful with a measure of success along the way, that's living. I can't end this little article any better than finishing with the ending with which our Wiseman finished his thesis. "Meaningless, meaningless, says the teacher, everything is meaningless... here is the conclusion of the matter. Fear God and keep his commandments for this is the whole duty of man." (Eccl. 12:8). On one plane, twentieth century philosophers have come to the same conclusion. On the human plane, life appears meaningless. That is why so many of us have lost the thrill of living. However, if you can take that one leap the Wiseman did, that there is a Higher Power and there is such a thing as life with purpose then meaning returns. But that's a story of its own for another time. We can leave with his thoughts on a physical plane of existence (and the spiritual one for another time), "So I saw that there is nothing better for a man than to enjoy his work, because that is his lot." (Eccl. 3:22). So what is that work, that lot, for which you were meant and have yet to fulfill? Discovering that is exciting. Find it and the thrill is back!

Chapter 11

Living In Our Final Years

Books on success are quite prolific but what I've found more difficult to find are volumes on successful living in the later years. When a seeker is younger, life offers endless options- career success, family possibilities, so many possible choices and so much good advice. However, when one's life journey has an end in sight, there are far fewer options and advice appears to be quite scarce. Whether one is in his late fifties or retired from active full-time work or one is beginning to feel aches and pains of a body driven for more than 300,000 miles and will never be able to be refurbished to be like new again, this is a time for reassessment. "What do I do now?" we ask. Is now the time to admit, "I've had a good life, had a good career, is now the time to just relax and enjoy leisure?" Or are we in the position to belatedly complain, "Now that I'm older, life hasn't gone quite as well as I had wished, is there anything I can do now, at this late hour to see an ending on a happy note?" What I envision is the need for a primer giving advice on life's Second Half or maybe "The over the hill" years. Regardless of how I lived my First Half, satisfied or not, what might I do now to ensure my life will end well? As I've written in an article on approaching the Second Half, there aren't as many expectations. During that first half we're expected to settle in a career, find friends, build a family with children perhaps and eventually feel we have established who we are and started to like how we turned out. Now during our later years, the question is, "What do I do now? Do I rest on my laurels? Do I start over? Is there a preferred path for the later years?" My adamant conclusions are, yes, there is an established path for those years, just as there is a set of expectations for a traveler's first set of endeavors in living, there is definitely a set of expectations for one's final years, so if you, the reader, are embarking on those later years or you want to flesh out a picture of what is in store for that time when it comes, this article will be a great place to start.

I think the first thing you'll want to know if you're going to spend some time with me, is how do you know whether your time is worth spending here? With all boasting aside, I can say I have the credentials, the life experience and a track record of successful living to substantiate my credibility. I have spent some fifty years now working as a theologian/philosopher. I've also a trained as a social psychologist with a PhD in Sociology and practical training as an MBA graduate. These areas of study have been my passion for all these years. What I treasure more than my academic credentials is my wealth of experience gained from well over fifty adult years of practical living. I have made my share of mistakes but nothing so egregious as to nullify the work I have done. Having studied, trained, researched my fields continually for all these years, I do admit I have had to change my views multiple times in order to come closer to beliefs and practices that are closer to reality. I am not afraid to admit my mistakes and reorder my strategies so they hold up to practical application and testing. Finally, though failing often I have had far more success than failure in the life areas that really count. I've had an idyllic marriage to my best friend for over fifty years. I have three children who I am extremely proud of. I have owned and managed multiple businesses that have been very successful. But I am most proud of the insights into living that I have discovered through study, discussion and active hands-on research for all these years. Some of these insights I hope to bring to the table in this piece. I do not take credit for all these discoveries. They are a collection of insights from other scholars, researchers in various fields along with my own personal research projects, intuition, endless reworking of ideas and the inspiration and driving forces of a higher power from the universe I call God.

Many of my readers may still be completing their First Half assignments set in front of them and others may be actually in life's Second Half or even in the Final Phase of living. If we have not completed discovering why we are here, that is our crucial goal before all others. To feel settled about our life existence, we really need answers for why we are here. Who am I? What am I proud of about myself? Am I pleased with who I am so far? Who are my mentors to whom I have turned for guidance and trusted through my life course? I submit, before we are done with our lives, if we do not have personal answers to these questions there will always be the sense that something is missing. Finish the unfinished business before moving on. (Please read my observations on navigating Life's First Half, in another of my articles for suggestions on how to find answers.) Wherever we are in Life's Journey, this learning project is primary and crucial. This is the foundation on which we build the rest of our lives. What I've come to recognize is that our Inner Being, or soul, consists of a number of aspects. We have a physical component, a mental or intellectual side, an emotional and feeling side and a spiritual aspect. Any area left unaccounted for, I found in my experience, leaves one incomplete. Even if we may not yet have a full understanding with answers for us personally, the most important acknowledgement is that we admit to our own selves we DO NOT HAVE ALL THE ANSWERS, but are searching. I am not so conceited or disillusioned to insist there is one answer for everyone, I'm not that all-knowing to say. But I do know we must have a working hypothesis to live by for optimum success. What I mean is, one should at least have an idea of what she wants to attain in life. How can anyone get anywhere without knowing where she wants to go?

We cannot know ourselves if we cannot answer, "What life experiences have I lived through that helps me explain who I am at this point in my life?" How can anyone come to like herself if she did not know some of the basic facts about how she got to where she is? I have gotten to know many friends and acquaintances well enough to realize those that have made peace with whom they are before taking their last breaths are the ones who can pass on gracefully and with few regrets. Imagine living some eighty years and still not knowing who you are. That is the predicament of so many in this fast-paced world that does not allow them to take time to meditate on who they are. To what extent have they really lived? The fact that you are reading this is an indication that you probably have enough time left to finish this unfinished business. If we haven't gotten these self-questions answered, we do have a major job to do yet. If one were to retire from a fulltime job, answering who we are becomes our new fulltime job for however long that takes. Once we know ourselves, we then can access our sterling qualities and those we are not so proud of. But don't be too hard on oneself, we all have qualities, abilities or experiences that give us hints about our true "Being." We can point to these as a starting position. Most all of us can leave this physical world knowing we have, to some extent, tried to work on improving our humanity. No matter how far we've come in building a persona, we can feel pride in some area, but none of us will come close to completing that picture. There is always more we could have done or further we could have gone. I personally have always felt within myself that I have attempted to do my best in working to be who I feel I was meant to be. Whenever we start, even if it's in our final days, that has to mean something. One wonderful gift we can admit is each of us came into this world with very little but we did come with a conscience that can assist us in gauging how far we have come in building our life and how sensitized we have become to use our conscience to know ourselves.

I have attempted, up to this point, to affirm from a logical progression the need for a goal all of us can relate to. I have intentionally not mentioned the spiritual aspect of life. All of us, I would imagine, would like to think life goes on after our body dies, somehow someway. The fact that most people that have ever lived entertain the sense that there is more to life then the seventy or eighty years is an indication there is at least a possibility life does go one. There are volumes upon volumes that take this search from a religious and psychological perspective. Each seeker must decide for himself or herself how one will answer those questions. All I can say here is most all studies show that those who so believe in an afterlife are definitely happier and more settled about approaching their failing years than someone who does not believe in such a possibility. By not taking advantage of the prospect of calmer, more satisfying final years (as long as one would be willing to explore that belief) wouldn't it be foolish to summarily deny even the possibility of a benevolent God and an afterlife that is intended to right all wrongs from the past? Certainly, it would be illogical not to all least give it some validity. My studies and my experience have proved to me personally that the spiritual longing that most of us have would make a world of difference in living happily to this life's end. I can testify from personal experience that having the hope of a future life or even belief in a compassionate, all-powerful God has supported me through several near-death experiences with a peaceful resolution and all during those hard times my life has been meaningful and has contributed to the well-being of others. I mention with fondness the five months I spent in the hospital being forced to contemplate my destiny and demise. One of the reasons I survived, I am certain, is the fact that I had within me a feeling of calmness and a sense that my time here had a value. I valued the enjoyable and awesome experience I lived through and the wonderful friends, family and acquaintances I helped even minimally. I could believe if this was my end of life, I had so much to be thankful for. For me, I endured due to the solace I gained from my lifetime experience that proved to me there must be an all-powerful, compassionate life sustaining source. I believe in the hope of an afterlife that will eventually right all wrongs, but for me what is much more important is feeling I was able to commune spiritually with that kind, caring higher power. Having that experience has given me the confidence I can overcome any adversity with supernatural backing.

PRACTICAL ADVISE ON LIVING THE FINAL YEARS

We are now ready to go into details concerning our goal for our final years. I have attempted to build a foundation so we can deliberately move with confidence that the time we have left allows us to connect the pieces and fragments of our lives from different seasons we have lived through. Now we want to unify what we have learned and solidify what we've accomplished or wished we could have accomplished up to this point in our life survey. Several important generalizations can be made. First, though the first half was mostly intended to be about ourselves, the second part is to be more about those outside ourselves. This is the time for giving more than receiving. This is the season for deciding on the legacy we hope to pass on to family, friends and our contribution to God's Kingdom and His universe. This legacy can include physical assets but more importantly the memories and encouragement linked with us. Second, I have learned from experience that every club, every conference, every planning group and every family needs elders to bring a measure of maturity and balance to the collective. I have found the younger members of a planning group bring the excitement and exuberance to move forward with the project, while the elders bring the experience to suggest what may be the difficulties to anticipate, the reasons to plan in more detail before jumping unprepared into the project. I frequently find myself listening to creative ideas propounded and saying to myself, "Been there, done that… this won't work unless…" I was wise enough in most cases not to blurt out why it won't work and thereby throw water on the excitement. I've learned to suggest, "That's an interesting idea, for it to work we need to think about this and that…" At least I feel needed and can bring a valuable perspective to the table. I'm still here for a reason. Our society will always need mature contemplators to pass on life's truths from real experience, not just theoretical prospects. I find I can shed light on what is most important and bring into focus the "Big Picture" to younger participants. They are needed and I am needed too. Look to join groups that could benefit from the presence of more elders and their perspective.

Furthermore, the later years are the times for meditation and finally establishing meaning for one's life. Finding meaning does not take much action at this point, but it does take reflecting. Engaging in reflecting or contemplating finds a perfect time when one has little strength but does have hours to think. It is only by contemplation that a person grasps meaning. Reflecting on a life time of varied experiences is how we gain wisdom and pass on wisdom. This is the ideal activity when we can no longer give a hand by virtue of our waning physical strength. I remember there once was a period when I had the physical ability to help friends move from one apartment to another. I remember fondly the time a group of fifteen guys including myself descended upon our church parking lot on a Saturday after a two-foot snowstorm so we could have a church service Sunday with adequate parking and that was back when few people had tractors in the city so we shoveled by hand. Probably more satisfying was the time I organized a service day at our church when we removed old seating, washing and painted all the walls and brought in brand new chairs for the service on Sunday. I had the physical capacity to volunteer my efforts for the welfare of others. I can no longer labor in that way but I still do have the ability to go to church regularly and, just by my attendance, greet others around me to encourage and commiserate with others. I realize that this is what I'm meant to do at this season of my life- to encourage, to pass on wisdom and by my presence contribute to group solidarity. I'm busier than ever trying to do good. Every time I catch myself feeling sorry for myself because of not being able to do the meaningful physical projects I used to, I find myself wanting to slap my face and lecturing myself about being ungrateful that there are still plenty of projects I can get my hands dirty in. Finally, as I stated earlier, the First Half on Life is about finding self, learning to like self and preparing self for future assignments that only someone with a particular type of life experience could do.

But the Second Half is for giving of self, sharing oneself, thinking of others and doing good for others.

Now here are the most astounding ideas I have learned for this latter season. First of all, I'm shocked to think this one thought I am suggesting never passed my mind in all these years previously. Yet, when I really needed to understand the concept of living in elder time, the fundamental principles came to me at the right moment, at an opportune time. And this pattern of timing is in itself one of the ideas I'm trying to pass on through my observations. I have found whenever I've needed ideas or directives, they have come to me by reading something somewhere, talking to someone with more experience than I or gaining an imaginative insight or intuition from within. I find I often get what I need when I need it. I cannot believe that I am one of the few this happens to. I'm no more special than anyone else on this planet. If I am guided along, why can't everyone else be so guided? I think part of the problem is most people have never come to realize this is one of the blessings God desires for everyone. The problem is, most people don't think to ask him for help. If you don't ask, you don't keep on the watch for the answers when they appear mysteriously (word used advisedly).

THE PERFECT EXAMPLE OF LIVING ONE'S FINAL DAYS

So let me tell you about the most astounding thought I learned rather recently. I have always recognized once I became a Christian that Jesus set the perfect example for humans, there is no way anyone could improve much on his life of piety and doing good. I have underlined pages and pages of Bible verses of his insights on living in this world along with pages of examples of actual events described by eye witnesses I use to model my behavior after. Little did I realize Jesus' final days set the pattern for how I should live my final natural life! Note that Jesus' "last days" were not the results of old age or disability yet Jesus sensed when those days were at hand. He knew when his work was coming to an end. He knew there was a last task to be fulfilled in this earthly traverse, to freely offer his life as a sacrifice for all humans. The marvelous thought I was given, passed on by others, is that I need only observe how Jesus lived his final days and pattern my final life course choices after his. Yes, I don't have the luxury of foretelling when my final days will come but my body, my mind and intuition hint those final days for me may mean days, weeks, hopefully many years. Yet I know that event is inevitable. What I must do with my time left is what Jesus did with his final days.

I always wondered why when Jesus was hauled into two courtrooms to plead his case of innocence, at the very least, I would think Jesus would have used that final opportunity to give his greatest sermon, the one to be remembered for all time. When Jesus was before Pontius Pilate and was asked, "What is truth?" (John 18:37-8) Jesus declined to use the opportunity for an expose' on the TRUTH. When Jesus was dragged into the chambers of King Herod, Jesus was again very passive (Luke 23:7-15). I never realized that within several days Jesus completely transformed his behavior. I never could understand that. Now it is clear and just in time for me to employ in my final life season, however long, I can begin practicing this final lesson and his example. Jesus transitioned from being an active, exuberant evangelist to being a passive and calm pacifist. He changed his behavior because circumstances had changed. For Jesus, this was not the time to fight back against the inevitable. He was to die; he was already convinced this was to be so he passively submitted to the final passionate outcome. Remember, too, when Jesus was taken captive and hauled before the powers that be, Jesus did not fight back. Actually, he rebuked Peter for being active and aggressive in taking out a sword to defend his Lord. Jesus is teaching us, you and me, there is a time for passivity.

It seems clear what Jesus is teaching. He is intimating to me, "Paul, you know what you are here for. Submit to it, do not fight it. You began this journey, some seventy years ago, now, calmly, passively go into your final act, your Act III so to speak, with confidence knowing what you must do. Whatever you do, do not give up or give in at the last minute, whatever trials may be ahead." And I am responding, "Yes, OK, I must finish what I started, just like you, Jesus. I know what I've got to do. I recognize I only have so much time left to finish what I am here to do. God forbid, the worst thing I could ever do now is to act in some way that would negate any good I have accomplished up to this point." I know and you the reader, when your moment comes will want to know exactly what needs to be done in your remaining time. Though we are constrained, like Jesus, to act less actively, in our cases maybe due to health constraints and other limitations. Yet we are to go forward with a more passive demeanor, no doubt accomplishing less in QUANTITY but now putting the emphasis on QUALITY of life. Following Jesus, we must reserve space to put in order all we must do before our allotted time is gone. And we put in order by preparing to hand over anything we have of value, accumulated time, treasures and talents originally entrusted to us. Further, as stated, the worst possible course now would be to actively do something that could nullify our legacy to the next generation. If we can do no more than passively exist in place and time, that is a testimony, in itself, to the validity of Jesus' example, his advice and his guidance and energizing spirit. Our faithful presence in the land of the living is the main testimony required of us in our last days. We are proving the truth that anyone trusting in him will find meaning, fulfillment, satisfaction and happiness beyond all we could ever have imagined even in this life.

MORE INSIGHTS FROM THE LORD

Let me pass on a few more insights gleaned from Jesus' farewell days. I will also be providing one more exemplary story I witnessed personally proving the accuracy of Jesus' message on how best to finish one's life course. This other case study comes from a most unexpected source, one very close to me, but I will leave that for later. Sooner or later we all will be hit with the notion we are not going to be around these parts forever. When that happens it will require a personal review of what is more important than any doing and even any doing for others. I fully came to that realization of this when I was in my latter fifties. Till then I was too busy to give myself permission to begin thinking about a time when I would not always be present with family and friends. Then, very surreptitiously, aches and pains began to nag at me physically and mentally and emotionally. I, for the first time, was forced to accept the truth about finitude. So, for me, that was after having lived almost two-thirds of a normal lifespan with little more than one-third left. I guess it might have been a little nicer to come to that awakening a little sooner, maybe half way through my life course would have been nice. Fortunately, I finally accepted the facts. And this is when Jesus' teachings on our human final days became more relevant than ever. His directives to his good friend Martha came back to me to ponder as a good example. Most of us know the story of Martha who was so busy thinking of Jesus and his company of friends brought with him that she centered her attention on offering comfortable accommodations and preparing dinner for all. She let slip what was much more important at the moment. She was too busy doing and that clouded her thinking. Jesus, of course, observed by his famous words, "Martha, Martha, you're worried and upset about many things, but only one thing is needed. Mary has chosen what is better." (Luke 10:41-2) Per Jesus, better than doing is contemplating and meditating at the proper time. That was Jesus' simple priority. Spend as much time as necessary in contemplation and meditation rather than doing things, even laudable things.

Especially if we have not spent many waking hours thinking about who we are, where we are, why we are, these might be the priority topics for life's final chapters. And just in case we are still too busy, life has a way of getting our attention sooner or later. I don't know if it is a coincidence but hours at home or elsewhere spent resting and convalescing from health issues is a "convenient" time to do the mental and emotional work if we have not gotten the answers to life's questions when we were younger. Our latter years, when we are prone to sickness and lower strength seem to have come at that convenient time. There is nothing more important, before it is too late, than finding what might be missing from the life we are living. Should we not realize our society is living the "Martha Syndrome?" We are kept so busy, with our jobs, with providing for families and then rushing to find occasion to relax as a breather from a jam-packed schedule, we never have the chance to stop and pause for answers to start flowing to us. Ask the average person if he or she is happy and you will get a tepid perfunctory reply of "I guess I am," without even a second to stop and really ask, "Am I really happy?" What more important project could there be if we put off asking such questions? Rather than looking at old age as a cruel intrusion on a busy, habitual even frantic life, as I caught myself starting to drift into, rather, look at these years (and hopefully they are years and not just days or months) as the period to prepare for our finale here. There is a big question that might be queried. Is it possible my death, once I am gone, could actually bring another blessing to my family, friends and community as I hope my present life has? Is there anything I can do now so that my death brings a further gift to those I love and care for? Those are my wishes. That may be wishful thinking, but I am an optimist, I learned that from Christ. I do not know how or in what way but, just as in Jesus' case, I wish my ending can be a beginning for others. We will talk more about this later, but for now, be thinking about those questions just mentioned. The answers that come to us privately over time may actually make the days we thought would be the days we thought we had the least resources within for us to give, to turn out to provide our very best contribution to others.

Not only did Jesus give us this advice in words, for it is not like him to just tell us, he always shows us, by his actions. He came to display how to live and love, yet more, to show us how to die! I mentioned, I never thought of this concept till I stumbled onto it just in time. That is often the way God seems to act. I like to think I find answers just in time for when I need them the most. I think that is true for many of us but sometimes we are just not aware. Jesus' advice and example extended the concept proposed in Ecclesiastes (3:1-8) centuries before. The wise man of old noted, "There is a time for everything under the sun…a time to live and a time to die." Yes, but Jesus took this a step further with his life example. Put clearly, there is a time to live actively and a time to live passively. That is just what Jesus did. He accomplished so much in three and half years by toiling beyond human stamina. Even when he was resting, he would actively pray and meditate. He actively did more in those few years than most humans could in a dozen lifetimes. But there came a time when he demonstrated passivity at the end of his life. Many of us may not have registered this subtle change in Jesus' manner starting at the Garden of Gethsemane. In the past when Jesus sensed his enemies were about to pounce on him, he actively "got out of Dodge," so to speak, left his community till the coast was clear. Not this time. Jesus passively accepted his fate. I had often wondered why Jesus, when he had the perfect audience, passively resisted taking a seemingly perfect moment to pointedly address his audiences of influential leaders when captured.

The salient point Jesus emphasized for us is that when he foresaw his demise was eminent, he made peace with what was the inevitable. For we humans, before our end arrives, the first lesson we are required to accept and make peace with is that. We admit we will eventually die and we accept the fate with a mature countenance. Our society tends to want to deny the biological facts. Judging by the myriad of surgeries and face-lifts advertised, patients appear to want to trick themselves into thinking they can somehow put off the inevitable. That is not what Jesus taught. When the time had come, Jesus made peace with his destiny, he accepted it without doubt or selfish sorrow. His understanding of what was at stake with his death and his willingness to suffer allowed him to feel and exude peace from his inner being. This peace is what is described elsewhere as "The Peace of God" (Philippians 4:7). To me and to many others who have felt this peace, it is a pure calmness that enwraps the whole body, every organ and every vessel, like taking a deep breath and a sigh of relief that permeates both body and mind with a sense of unquestionable security and a tingling sensation of confidence coming over the recipient. This sensation is the feeling all of us would love to possess throughout what for some of us might become an uncomfortable, even painful ordeal. Reading the biography of Jesus' final days, the reader is struck with the abrupt changes in his demeanor from his forceful and clear farewell speech to his Apostles, then to his calmness and passivity when he allowed himself to be taken a captive. Jesus had made his preparations ahead of these events so his actions beforehand set up a chain of events that took no unusual manipulating when he was suffering through his final ordeal. All that he had to bring to his last days was his faith, his staunch resolution not to deviate from his chosen course and his reliance on the Holy Spirit to give him superhuman endurance. The same is true for all his followers. As long as we approach our final stand, whether it be days, months or years, with a resolute spirit, after having made peace within ourselves, our God and our family and friends and peers, we are able to live relatively passively from that point on. Beforehand Jesus took similar steps to leave little for chance. He made arrangements for his mission to be carried on by his disciples, he gave out assignments and bestowed blessings so he could passively accept his final fate. The same for us, we do what we can to make arrangements, see an attorney for a final will, talk to family about final wishes and anticipate enjoying time left always praying that we will accept our future with the hope that somehow, some way our death will bring more blessings to others, especially those close to us.

I have consulted with many small business owners and have been nonplussed to find many of them have never given a thought to who will take over the ongoing company. Such an attitude is not only clearly selfish to family and employees but a foolish business practice. Just a little forethought would allow employees to keep their jobs and the family would receive extra funds to weather the loss of one of the family's breadwinners. Though I am not usually so blunt in counselling my clients, I cannot believe a person who claims to care for his family would leave money and other considerations on the table that could benefit the family and yet claim to be a caring person. Truly, whenever a believer puts the welfare of another person of equal importance to his own welfare, unforeseen benefits are derived. Some of my clients found once they sold their business, those funds either assisted them when they could work no longer or provide for their families once they were gone. This is what Jesus did. He thought ahead about all the details he would not have the time or freedom to put in order at the last minute.

THE SPIRITUAL ASPECT

An astounding set of discoveries appear when we conscientiously take steps into the unknown and unique world of passive growth. One will discover what the Apostle Paul did. As we mentioned earlier, he boasted of the Lord who made him, "strong when he was weak." This is one of those major principles for living that usually only a spiritually attuned person comprehends. For many, only when they grow into advanced years do they understand this mysterious riddle. Can you understand the meaning? Paul, the writer, used the word "weak" to stand for any type of weakness- physical, mental, emotional, spiritual. However, by late middle age, most individuals start feeling physical pain and more limited mobility and are reminded almost daily they must be more tentative with their health. At this point, a person welcomes any assistance and is more open to searching for remedies and his humility to accept help allows him to be more open to remedies that may result in his strength returning. When the Bible speaks of weakness the term is applied to many different types of weakness. Blessed is one who can begin to comprehend the far-reaching implications of this simple phrase. I have talked to many individuals suffering from depression, for example, who lacked the emotional tenacity, let alone the physical capability, to get out of bed each day. As a result, they were open to any suggestions to help. Usually someone who does not give up seeking guidance will find an answer, whether the answer is from physical medicine, psychological therapy, nutrition, exercise, so many possible routes. But one might have to methodically try every one of these options and more till one finally works; do not give up! For me, meditation and prayer have worked well to bring excitement, motivation back into my lifestyle. Having experienced weakness of all types from various causes has force me to analyze the possible underlying events or contributors leading to my feeling lethargic. Following my analysis and making a few small adjustments, I was surprised to find I could still experience, much of the time, the strength I had had previous to my lapse into weakness.

The apostle, writing from experience, found the greatest source of strength came from a spiritual force. When he could not find a logical solution through reasoning, could not win a bout with his physical ailments or when coming to a dead end he could "go outside the box," going beyond the physical realm and sensing a spiritual world of intuition. Spirituality includes intuition, imagining and sensing outside influences and accepting improbable "coincidences." These gave him (Paul) and us an additional avenue of fortitude including clearer purpose and resolution. I know if you, the reader, have not stumbled on this source of power, Paul's experience may seem too far-fetched to even consider. However, there are millions of Christians and no doubt millions of others who are spiritually minded who have experienced exactly the same sensations as the Apostle. I, myself, am one of those. Every year circumstances arise that I cannot find a reasonable solution for. It seems like it occurs almost monthly. So, I pray, and again, this is how SPIRITUALITY WORKS FOR ME. I first try different ideas that pop into my head. If this does not work, I keep searching for answers, and mind you, sometimes it takes months before someone, some article, some event shows up to give me a viable answer. "Thank you, Father," I say and try to be ever reverent for the help given me. This will never work for you if you don't at least try it. But trying means putting effort to give a reasonable attempt with an undoubting, believing heart where you are certain a solution is possible. If fact, Jesus' own words caution, "You must believe what you pray for is possible," for this to work (Matthew 21:22). This was a major discovery that goes back many years for me. I have learned physical and mental limitations can be a roadblock to answers. This is a real conundrum, understanding how weakness, when realized and not accepted as a permanent disability and when not giving up attempting will almost always lead to a path to circumvent insurmountable difficulties. Whenever we reach a dead-end or an impossible predicament we learn to get in the habit of repeating multiple times, "When I am weak, then I am strong." This affirmation really works.

As a person advances in years and if she has not learned the secret of spirituality, she opens up consciously and welcomes outside help coming from NO WHERE but actually coming from EVERYWHERE, to give the seeker a boost. I have learned God uses divine power coming from anywhere- a friend's advice, a Bible verse leaping out at me, an intuition, a threatening experience, a mistaken course of action, a motivational book, the encouragement from a mentor. These are all divine, inexplicable sources from a universe full of unfathomable resources available to all when one is ready to accept them. As one ages, the more fragile he gets or the lonelier she becomes, these people are almost forced to look for help when they admit to being weak. You might say this is a positive side to getting old in many ways.

Along these lines, I have always been entranced by the work of the psychologist, Abraham Maslow. He was the psychologist who, from research, came up with the theory of Self Actualization. He found if a person were not hindered in his pursuit of pleasure and security he would eventually seek and progress through levels of mental and emotional growth toward self-esteem and then self-actualization or human accomplishment beyond his own expectations. His theory is structured around individual human needs (A Theory of Human Motivation, Abraham Maslow, 1954). The human psyche is motivated by needs of the physical, mental and emotions sort. These needs include things like food, shelter, protection and once satisfied with those, a human will opt for a need to feel they belong by seeking out friends and peers. Next a person will crave a sense of self-esteem or self-worth and value. She comes to believe in her abilities and her contributions toward the betterment of society. If not thwarted at any of these levels of growth she will progress to her highest levels of fulfillment. Unfortunately, many individuals never progress beyond the level of belonging as a truly respected member of the community. They never reach full self-esteem and self-worth and therefore never attain Maslow's ultimate level of growth he calls "Self-Actualization." Being a scientist and artificially required to stick to exploring only the material world, Maslow never did take the leap and attempt to identify needs beyond and higher than the material.

Even though Maslow's world has its limits, his concept appears to be accurate. This explains why so many of us stop seeking to better ourselves beyond a preconceived notion that we are reaching our limit. Christianity, for one, teaches us never to stop learning, exploring, discovering and growing in capacity to improve oneself. Can we see when motivation to explore and discover new ideas, expand virtuous habits and strive to be all that one can be without limits, then theoretically growth never should end? Even when one is laying on his back twenty-four hours a day, he is still capable of praying, contemplating, meditating and inventing new ways of approaching life's issues. Jesus always motivates; he, in effect, says "Never say never," and always encourages keeping open to new possibilities and new outlooks. Keep that resolve to enthusiastically seek to improve. One's assignment while living is to keep growing. So many make peace with themselves, ask forgiveness from others or realize they have never sought the transcendental (spiritual) viewpoint and for the first time are sensing outside supernatural forces, energy and optimism flowing through their bodies. All this is possible even on one's death-bed. Personal internal work is never done until the work of breathing ceases. We are always needed for ourselves and for others till our last breath.

Where Maslow left off, without considering spiritual myster-ies, religious advisors have continued to connect the transcenden-tal and meta-physical to the material world. A simple transcendent theory was proposed by Robert Spitzer, SJ (Finding True Happiness -Volume I). He too speaks of levels of Pursuit of Happiness like Maslow but without shying away from the Spiritual. Spitzer posits a higher level of growth beyond the material and the world of appear-ances which he calls the Transcendent Level. I personally would add the term "Spiritual" here to capitalize and highlight a level of Desire and Happiness that suggests a realm far removed from the self-ori-ented outlook found in a purely secular philosophy. And again, I am not thrilled with the term "Happiness" as being the best term to describe what it is that humans are truly seeking. Maslow uses the term Self-actualization as being the highest level of human growth but the word "self" gives the impression of a limiting individual pos-session. I personally like to use the simple word "Fulfillment" as the essence of what humans wish to attain. FULFILLMENT includes pleasure and the connotation of Happiness and yet retains the tran-scendental idea of leaping beyond the "self" and adds the active sense of development that the word "Flourishing" contributes. This idea of flourishing is now in popular use to connote the idea of a human blossoming into something of astounding beauty. Either way, Spitzer is emphasizing the need for all humans to reach beyond the material world and beyond the limiting self or ego. True fulfillment and Full Happiness means stepping beyond the physical pleasures of this life (Level One of Spitzer) and the confines of the Ego world of the Self-centered desires of success and self-consciousness (Level Two) to the more liberating level of unreserved Empathy toward others outside of Self (Levels Three). At this point, a person has a desire to make a positive difference to the world beyond the self. This brings long-lasting happiness culminating in the Transcendental (Level Four) or as I prefer the Transcendental/Spiritual Level. This is the summit. An individual at this level of growth has the desire to give a helping-hand to fellow humans but also has the desire to reach up to the sacred level of the supernatural and feel a connection with God and His Universe attempting to be a force for good in a world that displays evil stains.

I would submit, as does Father Spitzer and all the Christian philosophers of the past (Augustine, Thomas Aquinas, Luther and including CS Lewis) that true fulfillment can come only when one strives for a connection to the community, society and the super-human world of Goodness and the Reconciliation of all injustice. Ultimately this is what every person wants to see once he or she has sufficiently explored the physical world of pleasure and the self-gratifying world of ego. All journeys, through many possible paths, ultimately finds a seeker at work for the well-being of others and a cause that spreads goodness and benevolence through out the earthly and super human realms of eternity.

Very interestingly, the foundations or bases of happiness or needs levels and all paths leading to full life satisfaction have been identified from ancient times. Both secular philosophers and religious sages going from way before Plato (400-300 BC) and the Bible (1000 BC) have identified these foundations as Love, Justice, Truth, Beauty and Longing for Home (or reaching one's ultimate yearning). All are mankind's ultimate needs and concerns. My studies, at least, confirm these are all unconditional values sought by most all civilizations, empires and clans. And these are the never-ending, never-extinguished values of all humans and especially those living in the Second Half of Life. Once we are satisfied that the pursuit of physical pleasures and self-inflating honors will always lead to a desire for more with no rest in aggrandizing or complete fulfillment in sight, we discover that only altruistic and those transcending desires bring the terminal satisfaction we crave. Our occupation in life's final years is the pursuit of what we come to determine is true Justice (fairness), Love (unconditional caring), Beauty (order, symmetry and wonderous sensations) and Being (an ultimate sense of feeling right with the world). These quests never end but are fulfilling in the meantime. Discoveries in these areas become more exciting and more momentous as time goes on. I find enjoying the stories and testimonies of others in their quests for these values is a fascinating project for a lifetime. The hope is that each of us, while still here, can contribute even a small legacy to the pursuit of goodness and the cardinal values suggested here. Rest assured we each can hope to make a contribution to the cause.

AN EXAMPLE DIRECTED AT ME PERSONALLY

I have one more model of Second Half and Final Years Living to present here. I am reminded as I write this that a great game especially in sports is often won in the last few seconds. This is why paying special attention to our final years or days are so critical. Accordingly, this is why I can not tell you about my final years. I am living according to the picture Jesus posted for us now but I will not presume that I will have my set of trials in the end. I have seen enough "nail-biters" in my lifetime to know a game is won or lost quite often in the final moments. A "Hail Mary" pass in the final one second of a football game or a final cry for forgiveness on one's deathbed are not uncommon. But I can relate another very personal life testimony very close to me to illustrate what Jesus teaches. This one concerns my son, Matt. He was not a well-known hero but to those who knew him he was a model of final year of life worthy of note. His life, for me, is kind of an enigma. Here I am a father learning from a son. We all learn valuable lessons in strange ways. I grew up while growing up to adulthood myself with my son, Matt, my first born simultaneously. I got married quite young so a good amount of my adult learning came in conjunction with raising Matt and as it so happens my late learning centers around him also. When I discovered from scripture what Jesus was telling me, telling all of us, as a model for our Last Days I only then discovered this other surprise. I had had a clear, real example of what I want to emulate myself. Everything I learned from Jesus about passive living, conviction, optimism and positive vision was demonstrated to me first hand by Matt. His life was cut short before age fifty. A little over a year previous he was diagnosed with AML leukemia cancer. Once diagnosed, he tried and we, his parents, tried every possible avenue to find a cure or at least a respite from the disease. We went to medical doctors, nutritionists, alternative medical facilities, we used every resource available and sought advice from anyone we could find who went through a similar diagnosis. The fact we left no stone unturned gave Matt assurance that all who loved him were doing all they could to support his fight. And as it was when he did die, we, his parents, sensed a calmness envelope us knowing we had done everything possible, with no regrets; we know and we knew Matt knew we spent a year of our lives giving him love and the center of attention, all we could possibly do. During that year of either visiting him in the hospital or taking him for treatment, that was a full-time job for us. Since Matt had never married, we, my wife Marlene and I, had him stay with us for the year and what a blessing that was. During that time, I learned from observation how a person in his final year might approach death and how to live knowing the end could come at any moment. I am certain by the fact Matt had been raised to think about the meaning of life and had been schooled in the principles of Christianity this was a major help to him. However, he was just a nominal Christian, like many Millennials and Gen-Xers, Matt did not go to church often, prayed but not daily yet he lived the life of a believer since he reasoned, from observation of his parents, that Christianity was a beautiful, viable and purposeful way to live. Having had the time to think long and hard about his predicament and a dire prognosis, he could sense how he must live. I interject this to admit there is something to be send about living by Christian principles regardless if a seeker is a Christian or not. Those principles really are effective.

Fortunately, Matt had a spiritual background when young and had religious training too, these principles appeared to flow up to his conscious mind. This is what I observed of Matt. During that year he had to live a passive life, he could only work at a secular job very sparingly. Keeping up a modicum of physical strength was a job in itself. Chemotherapy can be painful and will sap one's endurance. At best, he lived a passive life. Yet he kept his optimism and a positive outlook which was amazing to Marlene and me. He got up each morning with a smile on his face. He always looked forward to watching his favorite TV game show, Jeopardy, each night with his mother, Marlene. And while he still had strength, he would invite his friends over or would have his friends stop by to pick him up to go to a party or to dinner. He never stopped living though it was passive living. Through that last year he lived with the conviction he was surviving as best he could, always thankful for caring friends and solicitous family, never showing resentment to others for their health compared to his suffering. He had no enemies, never said a derogatory word about anyone that may have hurt him in the past. He had always lived with that attitude. So, though he was not religious, he was very spiritual in the sense of using his intuition and admiring the beauty and harmony of nature round him. I'm sure his training as an electrical engineer induced him to be aware of the order and balance in our natural world. I am still non-plussed wondering and trying to understand from whence his strength came. Whether it was that he believed in a loving God and felt no need to fear an afterlife with negative consequences or whether he had lived such a contented life in lieu of his personal share of suffering. In those first fifty years he had evidently done the hard work of discovering who he was, having apprehended his true self and lived, as I observed, without any ego pretensions. All these were possible reasons for his level of maturity. The point is, he lived the way Jesus modeled for all of us in many respects. During all this time, he was more of an encouragement to us and to his friends than we to him. He made that last year count! This is the way I am resolved to live my final times, just as Matt did, living with satisfaction and contentment, being thankful he had true friends and family, doing his part to maintain a close relationship with all, encouraging them, portraying a sense of confidence that he would do his best not to be a burden on others. And finally, he never stopped living. To the very end, he was active in learning, reading for self-growth and taking an active part debating on social issues, moral dilemmas and spiritual quandaries. Way to go, MATT!

What was true for Matt is true for any individual, and especially anyone who strives to be of value to community. One's living, even if sleeping the majority of the day due to health issues, is a reminder to all that here is a person who is of special significance. It may be with her presence among us the living, she is reminding us one day we will be in a similar condition perhaps and that engenders empathy within us. We, who may have many years ahead of us, are reminded to act now in such a way to have fewer regrets when our last fleeting moments arrive. We would hope our friend in adversity is given many defining moments of care and compassion during her struggle and we might ask if there are any final actions, we can take for her while still with us? However long she is with us can be precious moments for us who take the occasion to be aware of the scenario being played out.

However long she is with us can grant us precious moments to be aware of the scenario being played out. I was thinking, too, our society has a revered status for those who are young and active. The media acts as a cheerleader for all of us to strive to stay perpetually youthful. Yet, youth is that period when we expect to make mistakes and give little thought to consequences. Maybe with youth, one has the space to rectify mistakes, but the older you are, the less leeway one has to redo hurtful blunders; elders need to tread more cautiously. Experience in living should have taught us that while youth has benefits it has its drawbacks. Perpetual youth also comes with perpetual more opportunities for error, some irreversible. We would hope as we become elders we would act so as to appreciate the wisdom we have gained from experience which allow us to learn from our successes and past failures.

Furthermore, any individual, and especially someone who did strive to be of value to her community, has some reverential value while still alive. Her living, even if sleeping the majority of her time due to health issues, is a reminder to all that here is a person who has special significance to those around her due to her past efforts to care for and comfort others back when she was a vital, active participant in living. It may be with her presence still among us, she is a reminder one day we will be in a similar condition perhaps and will we act in such a way to have fewer regrets when our last fleeting moments arrive? We would hope she was given many defining moments of care and compassion and we might ask are there any final actions we can take for her while still breathing?

I have attempted to pass on a primer on how I am learning to live the Second Half of Life. I wrote here, giving thoughts and suggestions from someone who has lived successfully, contentedly and at peace in spite of my share of suffering. I can unreservedly present these ideas because they really work, time-tested and passed on by those who have lived such a life successfully with few regrets. This is the type of advice I was seeking and I believe you, the reader, feel the same way. We do not want theories or "maybe's" that perhaps this or that will help us through our last days. The ideas presented are all but guaranteed to help you navigate the difficult periods when they come. As a simple review keep in mind these ideas. First work to finish your "due diligence" from the First Half of Life. Learn to know yourself, to like yourself with all your good qualities and even your rough edges. Resolve you will continue to work on improving your integrity for the rest of your existence here. And when the time of passivity presents itself, simply follow the principles of Second

Half Living as we have already discussed. While there may be other paths that can navigate this period successfully, I can recommend the Christian way, it has worked beyond my expectations and has met the needs of millions of others through history. I am so amazed and grateful for the direction to avoid potentially harmful decisions I could have chosen if it were not for the guidance I received from whatever source, whether of human origin or from above. As a result, I am cautiously confident I will continue to do well during the times ahead of me. You may have noticed I haven't brought up the idea that this life is mainly a time of testing for humans. I don't like the word "testing" as if God is testing each of us as to how we will respond to temptations at this late period. As scripture says (James 1:13-5), "For God cannot be tempted by evil, nor does he tempt anyone; but each one is tempted when, by his own evil desire, he is dragged away and enticed." God does not test us; we actually have the opportunity of testing ourselves when we confront perilous events. I continue to pray for indications that I am putting my life in harmony with what I like to think of as a current of benevolent ideas flowing through universal consciousness. I have confidence I will have the divine Holy Spirit and the Peace of God to help me through any future ordeals. I realize till I take my last breath, one of my major projects will always be to enhance my virtues and godly qualities so I can work toward being a harmonious element in God's Kingdom (His vision of world-wide order). I know I have a goal to fulfill as Jesus did; mine is to leave the physical world having done my best to prove loyal and faithful to the cause I originally agreed to support. I am at the point of having all I need and want and am trying to put others, my family, friends and those who cross my path, with their needs on a par with my own. As long as I have the strength and capability, I'm still living to help others as I have been helped. And just as Jesus passively and without anxiety watched and waited for everything around him to be orchestrated to work without a flaw, I would like to think the same will be true for me. As Jesus did what was necessary in preparation for his end, delegating responsibilities, offering farewell messages and doing what is still possible, I am confident those I love will be cared for without me. Whatever any life to come consists of, I have come to know the Lord as the poem at Luke 1:49 confesses, "THE LORD HAS DONE GREAT THINGS FOR ME." I know the most powerful force imaginable is a God of Love. How can I have anything to fear with my life in the hands of a God of love? My search, I hope has helped me prepare for my disappearance. I also hope our contemplation together will encourage you, the reader, to do the same. I wish your Second Half and Final Stand can be approached with confidence and conviction.

Chapter 12

Purpose In Life

Over the ages humans have repeatedly asked the question, "What is the purpose of life?" or "Why are we here?" These questions only have meaning to someone who believes in a God or at least recognizes there is a spiritual aspect to life (i.e. believes in the possibility of something beyond the physical). If you believe life (including human life) just happened by chance, then these questions are probably meaningless. But please, read on.

If life just happened it would be nonsense to talk about nothingness having a purpose. Purpose becomes a moot point. As a result, Post Modern (twentieth century) philosophers have had the problem of responding to the question of purpose. So, permit me to take a couple paragraphs to give you the philosophical underpinnings before we get to the clear answers. First, many modern scientists' and philosophers' solution is to reason, "Since we don't know if there is a creator of life, then life is a chance happening and chance has no particular purpose associated with it. Therefore, if you have a need for purpose, you're on your own. The best you can do is construct or invent a purpose you believe is reasonable and try to live with that."

Such a solution really skirts the question by claiming these questions are irrelevant or at best unanswerable. Come on, there's got to be a better answer than that! Most people seek something more concrete. The fact that these questions of purpose have been propounded by millions throughout history is an indication that humans have thought "purpose in life" was a reasonable and relevant quest. If all societies known to anthropologists have pondered and suggested answers to life purpose questions, they must be relevant and meaningful questions that deserve further investigation rather than be dismissed as irrelevant or unanswerable. Why do these questions keep coming up unless they are relevant and there is a possible answer? Modern science has made incredible discoveries precisely by assuming answers could be found to logical questions rather than dismiss them as being irrelevant, as many post-modern philosophers or atheists have. If you are reading this, you, too, probably share the view that questions of life purpose are too critical to be put out of mind.

Pondering questions of life's meaning necessarily brings us into the realm of religion and philosophy and spiritual issues. This is to be expected since science's expertise is answering OBJECTIVE questions of a material nature. Questions of purpose and meaning are more of a SUBJECTIVE nature, the realm of philosophy and religion. Various religions since alphabets were first invented (circa 1800 BC) and philosophic works, especially the Greeks (circa 500 BC), have taken up the challenge. This is a worthwhile starting point. We can go to the holy writings of whatever religion one chooses for an official answer to the question. I, personally have found that Christianity gives me the clearest explanation and since this explanation seems to coincide with the logic of Greek philosophy, we actually have two major sources of knowledge in the Western World collaborating together. Both approach the questions from an individual perspective while most Eastern Thought is more focused toward a group or societal perspective. In this paper I will be reasoning using Logic and employing a few assumptions to start. This is not to say other avenues might not have additional ideas and perspectives to share but the Christian perspectives are so simple with no contradictions. The Bible began being written soon after our current alphabet was structured (circa 1000 BC) which includes the moral code handed down by word of mouth since at least 1500 BC. This is a good reason to start with the Judeo-Christian vision which has persisted with only minor modifications for three thousand five hundred years! No other picture has been so consistent for anywhere near as long! However, I've found some interpretations of these scriptures give pat answers like, "Mankind's purpose in life is to serve God"; that may be a simplistic answer but really doesn't give much direction to the seeker. I feel that by approaching the question of purpose logically first, Christians and other spiritually minded people are forced to construct practical meaning into their beliefs and will have clearer directions to follow. Also, asking this question of yourself first, motivates you to find an answer you can understand and use immediately. I invite the reader to follow a logical progression first and then supplement that with advice from a Christian or spiritual perspective.

A clear and simple introduction to the question of life's meaning was written by the philosopher, Aristotle, some 300 years before Christ. From this starting point we can add a more religious perspective to give a full picture of human Life Purpose and Potential. Aristotle laid out a logical progression to understanding the topic, regardless of one's religious or humanistic persuasion. He reasons on why Purpose in life is so important and then provides a logical method to evaluate that purpose in his Nichomachean Ethics thesis. There he suggests when we talk about Purpose we talk about function.

And just as a good horse, car, tool fulfills a purpose, the same must be true of humans. Also, he submits when we ask, "What is man's purpose?" we're inquiring about man's function. And just as we can easily answer the question of the purpose of a hammer by inquiring as to its function, we can do the same with mankind. Finally, he avers in living we need a purpose as much as an archer needs a target to know whether he has reached his goal.

As Aristotle suggests, let us pursue this question of mankind's function. So, what is man's function? He reasons that just as a shoemaker or carpenter has a proper function that can then be evaluated to discern whether he is a good carpenter or not, to conclude that "man as Man" has none is absurd and that purpose can't be "simply living …He shares that with plants." Aristotle reasons it's necessary to ask what separates man from other animals. Then he suggests our rational, thinking ability must be part of the answer and must be taken into the equation of mankind's purpose. No other known forms of life have this ability at the level of humans. Our purpose must be to use this ability to the level we are capable. I would also add, which the philosopher failed to mention, our ability to Love, by which I mean an unselfish interest in the welfare of others, is also a capability other forms of life are not able to reach. This too, ties in with our "mind" ability. Further, another aspect of human differentiation is man's spiritual aspect. The very fact we question "meaning" (which is not material) exposes that inherent spiritual side. And only with a highly developed mind are we as humans capable of empathy, the ability to reason how one would feel if he were in the circumstance of another.

Reason tells us we are capable of feats other forms of life are not. We have well developed minds; we are able to reason extensively and even have a sense of fellow feeling we call love. Aristotle concluded that if these qualities separate us from other forms of life, if we were born with these distinguishing faculties, our purpose for existence was to use these faculties to their full realization. Further, our purpose in life was to use our special gifts, perfect them, expand them and use them to a good end wherever they lead. He concluded that our highly developed minds, that we share with no other earthly forms of life, are a clue as to our purpose.

With this in mind, a Christian would reason thusly. Why is it we were made by God? What was his purpose for us? Was it to simply worship him? That's not really an answer, is it? If anything, that might be an answer to why we are in existence, an answer I think is questionable, but not an answer as to what our purpose is. Furthermore, it's rather illogical to think we were created to worship God since, by definition, God is self-sufficient. He would have no need for praise and worship. The only plausible reason for a benevolent God to create life would be to share the joy of life with others. Now, an indifferent or malevolent God might have as his purpose self-amusement, but most religions including Christianity reason that there is first enough evidence to conclude there is a much higher probability that there is a God rather than not and he or it is beyond the need for petty human self-centeredness. Once one satisfies himself that there is a God and that he is indeed benevolent, it follows God wants to share his pleasure and joy and profundity of living with us. Now we again ask, what is my purpose?

A Christian or any other person with a spiritual background also is furnished with another clue as to purpose in life. Christians are familiar with the concept of God as a benevolent, loving father. In fact, most all religions have discovered the tremendous practical power of love. They normally start with the idea that God is the source of love, and, in fact, the Bible goes so far as to say "God is love" (1 John 4:8). Just dwelling on that terminology for a moment helps us a great deal with working out life's purpose from a Christian perspective. All major religions have come to the same conclusion, that love is among the most powerful forces in the universe and that love is the basis of all benevolence and growth and progress in society. Rather than stall our discussion here while we reason on a definition for love, I'd interject that for practical discussion, love is at minimum an unselfish concern for others and their welfare. And since all major religions have independently concluded that God is the source of love (even Eastern religions such as Hinduism and Buddhism that conceive God as being the Universe itself and that humans are actually a little part of God still recognize that the Universe or God is the source of love), we can use this concept in our reasoning. If God is the embodiment of love, then He, by definition, is conceived of as interested in our welfare in an unselfish way. Arguing from the position of love, the major reason man was created by (or comes from) God was due to his concern for the welfare of others and to share his joy and pleasure with others. If that is true, what is mankind's purpose? God's purpose for mankind could not just be to have others glorify Him or praise Him, since that would not be a purely loving motive. Though those are ancillary results of God's sharing of life, they cannot be his primary desire (given that God is love). If God is love, He wants to share His happiness, joy and pleasure with others. Jesus was able to state in one sentence His perceived purpose in living. He affirmed, "My purpose is to give life in all its fullness" (John 10:10). A Christian takes this cue from his/her model Jesus Christ. Jesus' purpose helps illuminate man's purpose, to live life in all its fullness and to "flourish" in one's existence.

In my estimation many Christians have an incomplete picture of why God envisioned the notion of humankind, having the idea that

God wanted someone to worship him or to praise him. However, just a little bit of reasoning exposes that concept as a fallacy. Reason this way for a moment. If, as Jesus proposed, God is our father, we are led to a somewhat different position. Our conception of a father is one that loves his children. His motive beyond just procreation is to have someone to love, to pass on the pleasures and enjoyment he has experienced, to share. Reason would dictate that is precisely God's motive in conceiving of mankind. God wants to share the enjoyment, the pleasure of life, the ecstasy of existence with others. Our intuitive conception of God is one who is complete in himself. He doesn't need to create life merely to worship him. He's beyond that.

If we can only conclude that God's motive is love and love is more than just sharing, we have a notion of why humankind is in existence. God wants us to be joyful, to experience the pleasure he does. What an affront to our creator to look at life as a drudgery and an experience we are forced to endure. Yet that is the way some Christians appear to view the exquisite gift of existence. No, the Christian perspective is that our purpose is to experience, to enjoy, to relish life with all its beauty and diversity. Not that worship doesn't come into the picture, of course it does. Naturally we intuitively feel the need to express thanks for what we have been given. Naturally we're grateful for this undeserved and unimaginable gift of life. Mankind could not help but praise and acknowledge the unrequited love of our creator. But to say that worship and praise of our Maker is our primary purpose in life is putting the cart before the horse. Our purpose was and is to experience joy, happiness actually. Worship and praise are natural by-products of our experience.

Christianity reasons humans' preliminary search for purpose must start with the source of life (though Evolution theorists conveniently leave out the part about where they imagine the energy for the Big Bang came from). However, Christianity, from ancient times, and through its predecessor, the Judeo Version of the monotheistic concept of God, has taught the necessity of forming a relationship with this God. Simply by employing human intuition and the inherent moral sense of right and wrong and, yes, by divine intervention, truth seekers have come to know more about this God. Relationship with God is the starting point and the ending point. For a meaningful, flourishing and satisfying existence, a connection or a relationship to this source is the preliminary step.

When approaching a difficult issue all logical systems commence reasoning in a similar way. Christianity does just that by beginning with a logical set of assumptions to form what is called a "World View," an outlook to help sort out some type of order to navigate the journey. This tactic is much like how science starts with a hypothesis, an assumption, and then tries to verify or negate it. The apologist, Ravi Zacharias [1], asserts a World View must have answers to four levels of understand to be complete. He suggests there must be a determination of the ORIGIN or beginning point for that world view. There must then be some sort of MEANING visible for the scheme of things. And then there must be some form of MORALITY or moral code to assist in giving direction as to how to make decisions and how to live. And finally, there must be a DESTINY toward which to strive. Now, all religions do have such a complete set of elements to present a world view. In contrast, what some like to call "the religion of science," does not. Science gives us a sense of meaning found in logic and empirical observation and an unsettled Evolutionary Theory. However, it has not come up yet with the other three aspects of a complete picture. It offers neither a determination of the origin of the material world (before the Big Bang), nor a final destiny toward which the universe is striving nor even a complete moral code to live by. Science's feeble attempt at morality is the Utilitarian Principle that cannot come to conclusions on thorny ethical issues (discussed in most any book on Ethics). Yes, science asks us to have faith they will eventually have a system worked out, though they have been repeating that promise for hundreds of years. So, realistically, the only alternative is to pick a religious world view. The one I have found be most consistent, having a history of thousands of years of experience and a consistent ethical code, is Christianity. For thirty-five hundred years of written history and arguably hundreds of years of an oral tradition before that, all four aspects of its world view have not needed to change measurably. I have chosen to go with a proven, stable pattern for my life.

Christianity's staring point is a RELATIONSHIP with God. Having a connection with the source of life gives a constructive edge in understanding life's purpose. As an example, read 2 Corinthians 5:20-1. There, and in many other passages, we are invited to "Be Reconciled to God." The verses read, "We implore you to be reconciled to God. God made him who had no sin to be sin for us, so in him we might become the righteousness of God." We can only briefly comment on this idea here but any volume of Christian teaching will give you a good background. Suffice it to say that God is the personification of all that is "Good." He is conceived as the personification of all that is desirable, the perfection of Love, Wisdom, Faithfulness and Truth, on and on. Humans are anything but perfection and just like in a physical world, to join inconsistent entitles like oil and water which do not mix without an emulsifying agent, so the inconsistency of a perfect God and human error must be "reconciled." God gives the invitation but humans must avail themselves of His offer. The wisdom, understanding of our existence and the love, peace and harmony of life are opened to the seeker who follows this benevolent path to logical conclusions.

Furthermore, before one comes to know oneself and one's capabilities, hidden talents and gifts, a seeker must be settled in his or her understanding of reality. No different than any child needing to Mature. That is the first step. A relationship with God provides assistance in maturing physically, mentally, emotionally, socially and spiritually. And just as a child does not have the full mental capacity to comprehend complex issues of moral reasoning till she is a teenager, so one must grow to maturity in the five above mentioned capabilities. A relationship with The Source of Life will accelerate that growth and will allow one to comprehend issues hidden below the surface and access the wisdom to evaluate choice set before him or her. This process of forming a connection with God is the first step but not the end destiny of life. Scripture teaches our destiny is to be groomed to be true sons or daughters of God. This journey is best embarked on when one is young. However, anytime is an appropriate time to begin. An older adult who is mature physically already and with experience in living and having grown to some degree mentally, emotionally and socially may only need to mature spiritually and then might be capable, with God's guidance, to discern, in a short time, how he might use his resources to flourish in this life. Thomas Merton [2], the well-known monk, suggested many go through the motions of living but never truly live. He commented on how sad to think that many who have breathed life have never taken their position as genuine, unique God-Given Selves! Relationship is that important link. In my estimation, Relationship is not the end purpose but gets us to the end destiny.

In contrast, Aristotle [3] spoke of Happiness as the goal of life, or as purpose for life. I cannot be so dogmatic as he appeared to be. I question, still, whether it is happiness we are all striving toward or is our purpose something more specific as I alluded to previously. I admit the traditional Christian response is clear enough which claims I am in existence to praise God or I am here to serve God. But even that seems too broad and gives the impression I am only here for God's benefit. That does not follow in line with "The Epitome of Love," whom God is. All of scripture indicates to me God created mankind to share life with humans not just to have humans as His servants. Personally, I like to put the idea of purpose for myself this way. "I am here to become all that I am capable of being. My purpose is to become the true "Me," the one conceived by God. He graciously gave me life and I cannot help but feel subservient to Him. My relationship with God, as my Father, is as a son, not a servant. However, I cannot help but want to be his servant, voluntarily. But that's not my purpose in life. My purpose is to be all I can be, "The True Me." and as a result thereby radiate glory to God and make him proud of me. Am I making it clear? I am here to work on me first and the result is praise and glory to God, not the other way around. To me, Happiness is becoming who I am intended to be. Finding "The True Me" is the goal and happiness along the way is the indication I am going in the right direction. My musings tell me if asked of God, "Whose welfare is most important to Him?" He would say that is a non-question. My welfare, says the Lord, is the welfare of the universe, all creation, and God's welfare (a meaningless phrase to be truthful) is the welfare of Creation. All are synonymous.

I'd like to establish several other thoughts I think will expand our perception of purpose. As humans, we have inherent within us a goal-seeking mechanism like all other forms of life. We are constructed to seek pleasure and the optimum circumstances for growth and prosperity. But we have well developed minds and intuition (part of that spiritual aspect in humans) that set us far above other forms of life. Also, we are seeking a fulfillment that is open-ended, not closed-ended like animals. What I mean is if a plant or animal grows, survives and propagates and takes its place in the balance of nature, it fulfills its purpose. That purpose is clear and easily stated. A plant or animal seeks no more and no less. Its capabilities are limited and therefore its vision is limited. Humans are different, we have vastly more capabilities. With our minds we can imagine, we can imagine what could be, what we'd like to be and even imagine what others are thinking and going through. We can have empathy. There are so many more possibilities. That's what makes it so difficult to answer the question, "What is our purpose, what is life's purpose for humans?"

Aristotle's answer was happiness. The final purpose is "self-sufficient" in that it makes life "desirable and deficient in nothing." He calls this "Happiness." He felt all of us are looking for that elusive circumstance that will bring happiness. But Aristotle was quick to point out that what people think could be happiness may not be. Unless one uses his mind prominently in seeking and living this life of happiness, one would be accepting less than he could. He wouldn't be truly happy.

I remember at the time of my original study of Life's Meaning thinking, Aristotle didn't give me the answers but he did give me the encouragement to continue in my personal search. It wasn't long after that that I was leafing through a psychology self-help book at a book store that a phrase seemed to jump out at me. The simple term was "peace of mind". I realized then and there that was my personal answer and to this day I maintain that what everyone really wants, deep down and in the end, when all is said and done, people want to feel simply a sense of peace of mind about themselves and their lives. Let me tell you a little of what peace of mind means to me and you decide if that term is a synonym for happiness and is really what everyone is striving for. Peace of mind is more than just a clear conscience. It is a feeling of fulfillment within oneself. It's a validation of one's existence. My life has significance. I matter! Something good came from my being born. I can leave and I don't care about any rewards in an afterlife. I can tell God I tried! I couldn't do it perfectly, I couldn't love like You loved, I couldn't create beauty as You created beauty but at least I tried. I tried, at least sometimes, to make a difference, not all the time, but at least some of the time and sometimes I think I got it right!

Peace of Mind is a feeling that God permeates one's being, I've found. I can always console myself when I'm down, at least I'm trying, I'm really trying. That's the sweetest of feelings. I can sleep at night, I made mistakes today and maybe I didn't really try as hard as I could today but some days and maybe tomorrow, I will get it right. I know I have a place in society. I'm a productive member of society. I am aware of my relationships first with God and with my fellow sojourners in life and I know they are important. But one of the most important relationships is the one I have with myself. Whatever anyone else thinks of me, if *I* don't think I'm worth anything, what else matters? I'm trying, though, I'm not doing it perfectly and that's okay. The Bible reminds me that God himself said, "That's okay, that's why Jesus died for you, too."

This idea of Peace of Mind that I'm trying to describe is more than just self-esteem. Self-esteem is a feeling of competence. Though that's important, there is more to it than that. Self-esteem or competence gives you confidence in public but Spiritual Peace is a feeling within yourself, between you and yourself alone. I'm a genuine person, I'm the real thing. I'm trying to live as the real thing. I don't have to worry I'll be "found out". Confronted, I say, "Sure, I made that mistake and many others but I'm trying". "Most of the time my motives are pure," I can say. Now tell me honestly, isn't that what we all want? Isn't that the happiness that we all want to attain? I can hear some holy person (and I'm not using the term in a derogatory way here) say, "But isn't that a bit selfish?" And I say, "Yes, it is but isn't that exactly what you want?" Is there any sweeter feeling than the moment you long to hear, according to Jesus when before our Maker, He'll say, "Well done, good and faithful servant, enter into the joy of your Master"? (Matthew 25:21-3) Yes, that's what you want, too, though it may have a tint of selfishness in there somewhere. (See my treatment on motive in another treatise to clarify this).

When I understood the idea of Peace of Mind, for the first time I knew what the Bible means when it says, we can have "The peace of God that excels all thought" (Philippians 4:7). That's real happiness. I know what the saint that wrote those words really meant. And though I can't describe it fully (just like he admitted, it "excels all thought"), it's possible! I can testify to that special feeling from my own experience. And in the years that have intervened since Aristotle's time, there have been many millions of people that have testified as I have. Especially today, where we perhaps have more people living at one time who consider themselves genuinely happy than ever before in history, we have the opportunity to survey and learn from their experiences. Human progress has eliminated poverty for many, sickness for many, and opened doors for many. And what we've learned is that happiness is not an end in itself. We can never get to a place called happiness. Seeking purely happiness is elusive. Happiness is not so much an end or destination but rather a result or by-product. When you fulfill your purpose, you experience happiness. By the same token, once one is no longer living his purpose, happiness dissipates. So, yes, happiness is possible and in fact, is probable, but it's not what humans primarily seek. From my own experience and interviews of others over a lifetime, I have found the truly happy people are those who tell me what they really want is not so much happiness but fulfillment. They tell me they long for a feeling of doing what they like to do, seeking fulfillment in their lives by doing what they know and dream they are capable of. I can summarize what others have reported about purpose in a simple sentence, using the experiences of those who have lived a life with sustained happiness over a lifetime. I have not paid attention to those who in a moment of euphoria say they are happy. Everyone that wins the lottery says she is happy, she is excited but, in many cases, a year or so later, the happiness has evaporated. What is it that individuals who experience sustained happiness over long periods of time tell us? They say they are happy because they are doing something they enjoy doing and they are seeing good come from their endeavors. What they all have in common, the baseball player, the clergyman, the teacher, the metalworker, the carpenter and the homemaker is this: they are using their capabilities, whatever they may be, for some positive outcome. Humans strive to use the abilities they have, the abilities they excel at, whether they be entertaining others, creating with their hands, caring for others, building something of value (that could be houses, businesses or objects of art). Happiness need not be so elusive after all. What we really want is to feel fulfilled and that simply requires using what talents we have and to the extent we are capable.

What I'd add personally is that perfecting capabilities simply for one's personal joy does not promote long-term fulfillment. The lives of countless others prove that to us. Many, like Van Gogh, who painted pictures for his personal amusement only, to paint and not share with others, are not truly fulfilled. So, I'd add to the above summary by saying that a life that emotes happiness is one that uses and attempts to perfect his or her talents and abilities with the aim of enriching the lives of others around him or her. Furthermore, only a life that over the long term brings with it sustained happiness is a life that is fulfilling its purpose. So, while Aristotle would say man's purpose in life is to find happiness, we can go a step further and say a man finds happiness when he fulfills his purpose and that purpose is to use his abilities, his mind, and beyond his volitional mind, his spiritual aspirations and intuition to "flourish" given his life circumstances all for the good of self and others. I like to use the word "flourish", following the lead of a well-known secular psychologist, Martin Seligman [4] whose book FLOURISH used the term prominently and also by a Christian oriented sociologist, Christian Smith [5], who wrote "To Flourish or Destruct." They maintain that "Wellbeing" is best measured by the increasing of flourishing in one's life. They both came to similar conclusions I had come to independently. Flourishing gives the connotation of "blossoming," any entity coming to be an awesome specimen of beauty in its own right. A flower blossom, which when it opens, is a wonderful surprise that gives pleasure and meaning to all who come in contact with such extravagance. When humans "blossom" they radiate beauty, meaning, encouragement.

Before I conclude with a final philosophical perspective, I must add one secular perspective. Many years later, when doing research on a particular sociological project, I read some advice from one of the founding fathers of modern sociology (circa 1910), the German, Max Weber [6]. Having no vested interest and not in a position yet to make his own personal decision, he discloses his conclusions for secular sociologists. He averred everyone has but two choices with regard to meaning and purpose for one's human life. The first possibility is based on the fact that life is subjective and science is objective; there is NO way science can come to a provable conclusion as to a comprehensive set of meanings and life direction. Meanings vary among people. They are opinion and subjective. So, if one insists on employing logic and reason only in his search, he must and will inevitably resolve to live with no meaning and no provable effective goals. But there is a second choice. Choose a moral system that is logical and makes sense, though not absolutely certain, and then live by that moral code. Such a moral system gives one meaning, goal orientation, direction and comradery along with many other benefits. To me there is no question as to the choice I would make given the two choices. Others may decide to take Weber's first option and I certainly cannot condemn them but I really doubt that any of them can make the same claims as I have about my seemingly successful life path. As it was, I had chosen before having the advantage of Weber's eloquent summary of options. I take his words as a confirmation that my choice was logical according to his standards. I have not regretted any life chapter in all these ensuing years and seasons. I lived through many difficult ordeals but they were required to gain experience and learn lessons that excelled my growth to a level of maturity and wisdom I am grateful for now.

We close as we started out this essay by stating that moral codes are subjective. And as Weber demonstrated over one hundred years ago, purpose or morality cannot be proved with reason or otherwise; One must start with assumptions. Either one assumes there is order in the Universe and therefore at least a few concrete principles to create order out of chaos. Or there is no order and therefore one is totally on his own and logic, which requires order, is useless and why bother to make the effort. Our modern scientific world tacitly has made the assumption there is order and therefore presses on, though some scientists would like to have their cake and eat it too by alleging we will assume there is order but we have doubts about there really is any order. Either course requires Faith. That is what is being stressed here, ALL COURSES OF ACTION REQUIRE FAITH. Either Faith that there is order and presumably there is an author of the Big Bang or Faith that I can do it all alone, "I don't need anyone else, I'll figure it out myself."

For those of you who are Christians, you'll readily notice our reasoning comes to the conclusions the Bible sets as man's purpose. Jesus used the classic illustration of The Talents (Matthew 25:15-28). Back in the first century, a talent was a unit of money, but it's not just a coincidence that the term has come to mean abilities. As you may recall, Jesus spoke of three servants to whom their master gave each an opportunity to use their ingenuity to multiply the master's investment. One servant was given five talents, the second servant was given two talents and the third servant was given one. After some time, the master required an accounting of their activities. The first had doubled the money entrusted to him. The second did the same while the third returned the original talent intact with no gain. Jesus tells us the moral of the story. He shows that these talents were like our opportunities and capabilities in life. The goal, from a Christian viewpoint, is to use our abilities to expand the results valued by the Lord. Since we've already ascertained that God is love in Biblical terms, what the Christian God values is results that increase the love, kindness and welfare of others. In fact, scripture says the form of worship that is "pure and faultless is this: to look after orphans and widows in their distress..." (James 1:27) This passage shows from a worship of God standpoint, a concern for others is of paramount importance. Though worship is only one part of life, the point is clearly made. Man's goal from a Christian standpoint is to identify and then cultivate the abilities and circumstances given to each of us in a way that promotes the welfare of others and ourselves. And as Aristotle reminds us, those capabilities must of necessity include using our minds and as I would hasten to remind, human minds allow for empathy which is a precursor to love. Some may have more "talents" or abilities than others but the Bible encourages comparing ourselves to ourselves rather than to others. The master in Jesus' illustration was just as proud of the servant who increased the wealth from two to four talents as he was with the servant who increased the wealth from five to ten talents. Christians follow Christ's example of giving, sharing, helping others materially, intellectually and emotionally, all this with the goal of promoting a better world in line with God's intentions. From a practical standpoint then humans can fulfill their purpose in life by first identifying their gifts, then perfecting those gifts and directing the benefits of those gifts to the world outside of themselves. By doing this, the individual captures a sense of identity and self-esteem, enriches the world outside of herself, automatically fulfills the Christian goal of glorifying God and simultaneously feels a sense of happiness (peace of mind) that comes as a by-product of her activities.

I encourage you now to take the steps that will lead to a life of purpose with concomitant happiness (peace of mind). Your purpose in life is the same as mine, though the unfolding may be quite different. Simply ask yourself, "What are my special abilities, what have others who know me say I'm good at?" Once those special gifts are recognized, resolve to employ those talents in a career or avocation (hobby) that benefits others! Imagine what a flourishing life might look like in your case. Imagine how your self-esteem will soar with the unfolding of a fulfilling purpose! Then, rest assured, everything else of value, happiness, praising your Maker, feeling good about self, will all fall into place.

REFERENCES:

1. Zacharias, Ravi, The Logic of God, Zondervan, 2019
2. Merton, Thomas, The Inner Experience: Notes on Contemplation, HarperSanfrancisco, 2004, 4
3. Aristotle and Jonathan Barnes, Complete Works of Aristotle, Vol.1, 1984
4. Seligman, Martin, Flourish, Simon and Schuster, 2011
5. Smith, Christian, To Flourish or Destruct, University of Chicago Press, 2015
6. Weber, Max and H.H. Gerth, et al, From Max Weber: Essays on Sociology, 1958

Chapter 13

The Time Of Your Life

Many years ago I happened to go to a play. I heard a line that was so haunting and seminal that I never could forget it. Though it hasn't always been consciously on my mind, at pivotal strategic times it seems to surface, I'd pull out the line and reread it carefully. "In the time of your life, live- so that in that wondrous time you shall not add to misery and sorrow in the world but shall smile to the infinite delight and mystery of it." These are the words of playwright William Saroyan from this play, "The Time of Your Life."

I guess one of the reasons this quote was so haunting to me was that his use of the phrase, "Time of your life" is not the usual meaning that comes to mind. I remember the first time I comprehended his meaning I was taken aback. I recognized, though the words had a popular interpretation, his was much more profound and significant. Being young at the time, I was fortunate to be having "The time of my life," exploring, learning, experiencing, enjoying. The play startled me to realize consciously that "The time of my life" was a finite time. I vowed, then and there, to ensure the remaining times of my life would be lived appreciating while having the time of my life. I averred to have "the time of my life" during "The time of my life." The odd thing is that in all these years since, I've never once heard anyone use the two phrases simultaneously like I had to myself. It seems so natural, so simple. Yet if I were forced to use my personal life experience to come up with a directive on HOW one should live one's life, I couldn't do much better than to advise living life so that you use "the time of your life" to have "the time of your life."

Let me explain what I mean. It's obvious the two identical phrases have two different meanings. You go to an amusement park or rock concert to have the time of your life. That's an experience, an invigorating, enjoyable experience. To live or exist in the time of your life, we're talking duration, a limited span of time. When employing the first meaning the phrase anticipates a positive, exciting experience, the second usage may connote a somewhat depressing thought, reminding us that this life doesn't last forever. I personally feel I haven't truly learned two of Life's important lessons if I haven't come to comprehend the difference between having "The time of your life" (life enjoyment) and properly allocating "The time of your life" (the actual, finite time).

Let's explore lesson one first. What does it mean to have to have the time of your life? Clearly each of us will offer a subjective opinion on what the idea commutates to him or her. As a Christian I've come to believe we're each here to experience the time of our life. Optimally I should be able to look back on the time of my life with fond memories, to be able to admit, "Yes, I had my set of problems, my burdens to bear, but I also had many, many wonderful moments. I'd recommend this existence to anyone; life was worth the time I spent in it!" As to the subjective interpretation of "the time of my life," I realize I must tread carefully. For example, my personal idea of having the time of my life is not that of living in a third world country as a missionary allaying the suffering of others. I have good friends, though, who are having their times of their lives doing just that. However, neither is traveling the world to ski the slopes on every continent my idea of having the time of my life, and it's not just because I can't ski. Again, I have friends for whom that would be their dreams. When I look back, I'll freely admit that among the greatest times of my life were times spent exploring, learning, experiencing shared moments with others. I wish I could ask each of you personally what have been the greatest times of your lives. Whatever you do, cherish them, remember them, and revel in them. And then expect there will be more to come. I've come to believe "You're not really living unless you appreciate you ARE living." Simply being awake through one exciting moment after another, without taking a moment to reflect, to truly experience and be so thankful for the opportunity, cannot possibly produce maximum enjoyment.

A man who lived life to the full, and who experienced a life you and I could never hope to duplicate, had this to pass on. Writing in 1 Peter 4:2-6, he cautioned not to be enamored with the physical intrigue and pleasure of the material. He observed of a fully functioning individual, "He does not live the rest of his earthly life for evil human desires, but rather for the will of God...LIVE according to God in regard to the SPIRIT." What an interest expression, "to live with regard or in regard to the spirit." Peter is claiming, based on his experience, living is more than just living in a material world. There are things, experiences out there, we can't always literally see or sense. Life has a spiritual aspect that must not be neglected. More on "living with regard to the spirit" another time, but Peter is hinting you can't have the time of your life without connecting to the spiritual aspect of life.

Now for lesson two, which to me is the same as lesson one, but with a different slant. Time, in each turn of events we find ourselves, are moments to be collected and valued. Not that you ever want to live them over again, but these experiences are part of you, you wouldn't be quite the same person without them. The end product of your personal human life is a collection of a set of finite moments, experiences that molded you into the unique work of art and bundle of stories that make up you. If only we could appreciate that we've taken away within us something from each episode we've experienced. We've learned as much, maybe more, from the bad times as we have from the good times. Either way they're our times, the times of our personal lives. As humans, we only have so many of them. And you come to discern you can't always appreciate at the moment, while you're living the episode, how valuable it may prove to be later. What you discover, the excitement you feel, the beauty you share, are the exact same experiences you have in common and share with millions of others, those before you and those after you're gone; they are the connections that bind you to the progression of humanity.

Value each moment. Don't make the mistake of evaluating each moment at the spur of the moment so to speak. You don't know till all the little moments are collected which you'll cherish most. I've had others tell me as they surveyed their lives toward the end of their own finite string of days, "My most cherished times were the seemingly mundane times when I was a kid at home watching TV with my family, father, mother, siblings." Or "I remember so clearly when I was just lying in the grass on a warm summer day gazing up at the sky trying to make sense out of the shapes the clouds were drawing." Those are all parts of the time of my life.

I've come to value the admonition of the many Bible verses like the one at 2 Corinthians 6:2, " I tell you NOW is the time of God's favor, NOW is the day of salvation." The biblical sage fervently stresses the most momentous times of your life are the NOWs. The Now won't be repeated, it can never be experienced again in exactly the same way, it can't be taken back, and there are only so many of them. It really irritates me to hear someone admitting to deferring his or her living in the present for a future afterlife. "I'll wait till heaven to really enjoy life, that's when the real life begins." I want to blurt out, "What do you call this existence, just being conscious, is it to be treasured any less than being the most wonderful gift ever to be conceived? Is this time so trivial that it's worth so little to be squandered and not cherished? Don't you realize that one of the men who most fervently pointed to the joys and rewards of heaven exclaimed the words we just read,' NOW is the day of salvation'? Now is all you're guaranteed. Don't miss out on the NOW."

To me, having the time of my life means being able to revel in the exquisiteness of nature around me, marveling at what mankind has been able to do, his inquisitiveness and inventiveness, the joy of sharing with others, the satisfaction of doing something, anything, constructive especially for others and getting acquainted with my roots to the divine, my divine connection, my spiritual side and then sharing that discovery with others. Exploring, questioning, marveling, helping, caring, that's having the time of my life.

Finally, the author, William Saroyan had one more observation as he surveyed our collective time here, "In the time of your life, Live-so that in that good time there shall be no ugliness or death for yourself or for any life your life touches. Seek goodness everywhere, and when it is found, bring it out of its hiding place and let it be free and unashamed."

What a joy to read such words. They remind me that living is a magical time. There is so much to do, so many ways to show our concern for those we love and so many things to marvel at. There's just not enough of it, time. Let's appreciate that. I wish for all of you, my friends, that you too may have the "TIME of your life during the time of YOUR LIFE."

Made in United States
Orlando, FL
26 February 2024

44146826R00133